LITERATURE IN THE CRUCIBLE
OF TRANSLATION:
A COGNITIVE ACCOUNT

REVISED SECOND EDITION

DANIEL C. STRACK

UNIVERSITY EDUCATION PRESS

Okayama, Japan
2016

CONTENTS

ACKNOWLEDGMENTS ·· 5

NOTE ·· 7

1 IS TRANSLATION RELEVANT? ························· 9

2 THE NEURAL FRAMEWORK ························· 14

3 WORDS MAKING SENSE ····························· 24

4 THE REASON FOR RHYME ························· 50

5 WHEN WORLDS COLLIDE ························· 81

6 THE SQUEAKY WHEEL ····························· 108

7 NINE STATELY RAVENS ····························· 123

8 TRANSLATING AMBIGUITY ························· 157

9 SURVIVAL ·· 188

REFERENCES ·· 203

ACKNOWLEDGMENTS
(FIRST EDITION)

The publication funding for the first edition of this book was provided by the University of Kitakyushu—Faculty of Humanities Research Publication Subsidy. My thanks are extended to the University of Kitakyushu for this genuine research incentive.

I especially wish to thank Margaret Ho, Kinoshita Yoshisada, and Maeda Johji for their seemingly boundless assistance and understanding. It is not an exaggeration to say that without the support of these particular individuals, this book would not have been possible.

My colleague Craig Lambert offered many constructive comments on an early draft. Margaret Freeman, Yanna Popova, Reuven Tsur, Charles Forceville, William Benzon and many other members of the *Cognitive Approaches to Literature* online discussion group offered valuable information and insights. Zouhair Maalej was helpful in suggesting research on cognition and translation that I had been unaware of. I am also indebted to Benjamin Bergen and the other instructors and participants at the EMCL3 workshop who provided sound advice on various practical issues relating to experimental research.

Many of my colleagues at the University of Kitakyushu, far too numerous to name individually, offered advice from their areas of expertise. I feel fortunate to work among such gifted and helpful people.

I have greatly benefited from my involvement in the following organizations: the Japan Comparative Literature Association, the International Cognitive Linguistics Association, and the Japan Modern Literature Association-Kyushu Chapter.

I would also like to thank the many scholars and students (especially my metaphor seminar and translation students) who have sought to understand literature, linguistics, and translation, and have, whether directly or indirectly, contributed to my ongoing education. As I straddle various disciplines to write this book, I am humbled both by the tremendous insights I have had access to and the huge gaps in my own understanding that remain to be filled.

Daniel C. Strack

January 1, 2007

ACKNOWLEDGMENTS
(REVISED SECOND EDITION)

This Revised Second Edition of *Literature in the Crucible of Translation* primarily represents an attempt to correct multiple proofreading errors that, due to severe time constraints, were not detected during the editing process for the First Edition. My thanks go out to the many individuals who purchased the First Edition (thereby making this new edition possible) and also to University Education Press for their willingness to delay publication of this edition until revisions were completed.

While changes have been made both to amend errors and to clarify the logical flow of certain passages, no significant alterations have been made to the book's original content. The reasons for this are twofold. First, it was judged that any attempt to thoroughly update the First Edition would require comprehensive rewriting, partial reorganization, and extensive additional research. While publishing an up-to-date, expanded edition may prove valuable in the long term, in the short term such a reworking would clearly go beyond the scope of simple revision. Secondly, it is the author's firm belief that, while various new scientific insights that corroborate the ideas found in this volume have come to light over the 9 years since the book's original publication, the ideas presented here are as valid in 2016 as they were in 2007.

Daniel C. Strack

January 1, 2016

NOTE CONCERNING JAPANESE ORTHOGRAPHY AND PERSONAL NAMES

For consistency in transliteration and to aid those who hope to do further study, the orthographic style used in this book to express Japanese words and personal names follows that used in *Kenkyusha's New Japanese English Dictionary*, Fourth Edition (Masuda 1974), with a few exceptions being made for the names of individuals I know who prefer a different style of Romanization. Place names have been written in their standard orthographies.

In general, Japanese names in this book have been written according to the traditional Japanese order (surname first, given name second). I will refer to authors and scholars by their surnames, with exceptions made for Japanese literary figures including Matsuo Bashō, Nagai Kafū, and Natsume Sōseki, who are known by their pen names, Bashō, Kafū, and Sōseki.

1

IS TRANSLATION RELEVANT?

Sounds as well as thoughts have relation both between each other and towards that which they represent, and a perception of the order of those relations, has always been found connected with a perception of the order of the relations of thoughts. Hence the language of poets has ever affected a certain uniform and harmonious recurrence of sound without which it were not poetry, and which is scarcely less indispensible to the communication of its influence, than the words themselves without reference to that peculiar order. Hence the vanity of translation; it were as wise to cast a violet into a crucible that you might discover the formal principle of its colour and odour, as seek to transfuse from one language into another the creations of a poet.

Percy Bysshe Shelley

(1821: 141)

The title of this book alludes to Percy Bysshe Shelley's *Defence of Poetry*, Part I, from which the epigraph for this chapter is taken. Essentially, when Robert Frost commented that "poetry is what is lost in translation" (Untermeyer 1965: 248), he was saying the same thing more concisely. Translation is a process that seems to strip poetry of something essential. Whereas precious metals can be refined in the fires of a crucible, violets cannot. For Shelley, then, translation is seen to have the same effect on poetic works: the most important aspects are lost and so attempts to translate poetry are worse than futile, they are destructive.

Shelley's metaphor is intuitive and compelling and it certainly has an element of truth to it, but just how far does that truth go? The best way to find out is to carefully examine translation, both in terms of the translation process and its results. Such an examination will be attempted in this book.

Before proceeding, however, it may be useful to temporarily break away from Shelley's POETRY IS A FLOWER metaphor and reorient our thinking to a metaphor that will, I believe, ultimately prove more productive. The idea for the metaphor that follows has been gleaned from Andrew R. MacAndrew's translator's preface to Dostoevsky's *The Brothers Karamazov* (MacAndrew 1981: x). I have rephrased and adapted his metaphor so as to better reflect the order and content of this volume.

Imagine a symphony. Of course any type of music will suffice, as long as it is sufficiently complex. For the time being, though, imagine a symphony.

A conductor stands before a group of well-trained musicians, brings the baton up and pauses momentarily. During this pause, the audience anticipates the music. Perhaps they already know the composer or the work itself. Perhaps for some it is their first classical music concert ever and they do not know what to expect. The pause is only momentary and then the baton drops and the concert begins.

The musicians play various instruments which produce a broad array of sounds: percussion, woodwinds, brass, and strings. Each instrument covers its range, moving around the musical scale in various tempos and rhythms. Some notes are accented and others flow by. Here a crescendo, there a decrescendo. The musicians individually produce a broad array of sounds, often in parallel with other instruments but sometimes standing out and at other times fading into the background. And then it is done.

Probably nothing that has never happened before has happened during the symphony. No new notes have been played nor have any new rhythms been unleashed. If the symphony is thought to be interesting (and not just a lot of random noise) it will be because the listener has appreciated the combinations of patterns and emphases in the music. If the combination of musical elements is appreciated and has been worth the time spent in listening to it, the symphony has been a success, at least for that one listener. One goal of this book will be to show how literature succeeds, at the level of individual readers, in just such a way.

So how does this image of literature relate to translation? There are many kinds of translation with many different goals. Translating a user manual for an industrial steel furnace or a diplomatic treaty between two nations requires an understanding of the purpose of each document. If the end user of a newly acquired steel furnace can use it without incident then, functionally, the translation has been a success. If a diplomatic treaty results in peace and stability between the two nations then, functionally, that translation also has been a success. But what is the function of literature? How will we know when a literary translation has been successful?

In translating literature, it is useful to ask: "What are the literary aspects of the text to be translated?" If translators do not know the answer to this question, even vaguely, they risk producing translations which cannot provide an answer for the question, either. Of course, five translators may translate the same literary text and, in their translations, express five different answers as to why the text is literary. Each answer may be equally valid. The translator who plows ahead without awareness, however, will follow the path of least resistance. In translation as in life, the path of least resistance is often the road to nowhere.

Once the translator has an answer to the question of what is literary about the original text, there is an even greater challenge that awaits: how to take that literariness and express it in another language. Returning to the example of the symphony, how can we take the music of a certain composer who composed for certain instruments in a particular culture and express the same symphony with whatever instruments happen to be available in a different culture? In fact, translating is probably even more difficult than trying to rewrite Beethoven's 9th symphony for jazz quartet, polka band, or steel drum ensemble. Differences in language and culture make translation a seemingly impossible assignment.

Unfortunately, translation theory at present is ill-equipped to practically address such challenges. Although the study of translation has been taken up by scholars in many different academic traditions, with each tradition offering unique and useful insights, it is difficult not to agree with translation scholar Elzbieta Tabakowska when she observes that systematic and theoretically sound approaches to translation do not (as yet) exist (Tabakowska 1993: 2). This problem is compounded when the text to be translated is literary. George Steiner argues that those who claim to put forward theories of literature, criticism, or translation are simply bluffing (Steiner 1998: xvi). Admittedly, literature as an academic discipline has proven remarkably resistant to the idea that falsifiable claims must form the bedrock of any legitimate "theory."

Cognitive linguistics, to the extent that it recognizes the value of literature along with other social and cultural aspects of human cognition, is ideally situated to serve as a common scientific testing ground upon which the varying approaches to translation may empirically verify their claims. In hopes that eventually skepticism concerning the possibility of developing a theory of translation will prove unfounded, cognitive linguistics and neuroscience will provide the framework for assertions made in this volume.

Having said this, it is also true that information concerning the mind's processing of language is still being gathered, verified, and in some cases, debated. At present, it is impossible to say that all of the pieces of cognition which relate to literature or translation have been understood or even identified. Unfortunately, translators do not have the luxury of waiting until cognitive scientists reach whatever level of agreement they deem to be adequate. The everyday work of translation will proceed even without a cognitive account of what is happening during the process.

For this reason, I see no point in delaying. Concentrating on the information that is available and not worrying about the information that is not, I offer this limited "account" with the hope of contributing something of value to the ongoing research and theoretical debates. The time seems right to examine what happens to literature when it is cast into the "crucible of translation."

2

THE NEURAL FRAMEWORK

[T]here are about one million-billion connections in the cortical sheet. [...]
If we consider how connections might be variously combined, the number
would be hyperastronomical — on the order of ten followed by millions of
zeros.

Gerald M. Edelman

(1992: 17)

Translation-related skills and linguistic knowledge do not spontaneously develop when the translator views the source text for the first time to begin translating. Translation is always preceded by language and culture and so the ways in
which the brain's neural connections come about, the ways in which children
acquire increasingly sophisticated communicative skills, and the ways in which
cultural representations are perceived and manipulated must be accounted for in
any viable theory of translation. Just as general cognition sets the parameters for
language ability, general cognition and language ability in tandem subsequently set the parameters for literature.

As translation of literature occurs in a network where both of types of
parameters interact, it would be helpful to distinguish general cognitive parameters that effect literary understanding from culturally and individually biased
linguistic and literary preferences, if possible. This chapter will give a brief
overview of neural development so that, in chapters 3 and 4, certain key language-related aspects of cognition that affect literary values may be more clear-

ly highlighted.

Development of the Neural Framework for Language

Specialized cells called neurons form the network that accomplishes the various goals of the body by transmission of electrochemical stimulus. A prototypical neuron has three basic parts: the soma (cell body), the axon (an output fiber), and dendrites (input fibers). Neurons are connected to other neurons, forming electrochemical circuits that consist of "conducting wires (the neuron's axon fibers) and connectors, known as synapses (which usually consist of an axon making contact with the dendrites of another neuron)" (Damasio 1999: 324). (See Figures 2.1 and 2.2)

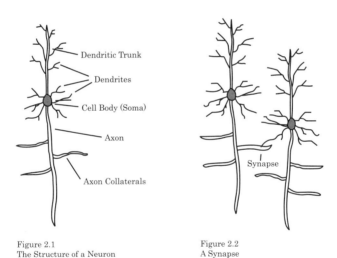

Figure 2.1
The Structure of a Neuron

Figure 2.2
A Synapse

Neurons generate nerve impulses that are called action potentials. While the action potentials of one kind of neuron may be somewhat different from those of other types of neurons, the multiple action potentials resulting from the firing of a single neuron are consistent in size and duration (Bear et al. 2001: 74). Generally evidencing greater similarity to a burning fuse than to an electrical charge (Bear et al. 2001: 89-91), these electrochemical impulses do not carry "information" (Edelman 1992: 27). The spikes (action potentials) generated by neurons are similar to the clicks of a Geiger counter in the presence of radiation; in response to strong stimulus a neuron fires rapidly and weak stimulus will produce less frequent or intermittent spikes. These firings are not in any way "encoded" and are functionally distinct from the highly calibrated succession of electrical pulses that travel along telegraph wires or through digital processing equipment.

The network of neural subsystems instantiates itself according to the basic cellular processes of division, migration, death, adhesion and induction. Although the timing of these events is coordinated according to genetic constraints, "individual cells, moving and dying in unpredictable ways, are the real driving forces" of neural development (Edelman 1992: 60). The overall configuration of the brain is genetically coordinated but from early embryonic stages, "neurons extend myriads of branching processes in many directions" and connectivity is established at the synapse level as a result of individual development (Edelman & Tononi 2000: 83). Neurons do not simply branch out to complete the system; a mature and functional neural system requires some little-used connections to be eliminated while more active connections are strengthened. Neuroscientist Gerald Edelman has called this selection process Neural Darwinism. Biological anthropologist Terrence Deacon notes, "[n]ature prefers to overproduce and trim to match, rather than carefully monitor and coordinate the development of innumerable cell populations" (1997: 197).

A neuron will only generate an action potential at the near-synchronous firing of many inputs coming from other neurons (Deacon 1997: 202). Furthermore, the magnitude of the input stimulus can increase the firing frequency of the action potentials; the more intense the stimulus, the greater the chances that a connection will be selected to "live" and become entrenched. There are two rules of thumb that sum up this neuronal selection process: "neurons that fire together, wire together," and "neurons that fire out of sync, lose their link" (Bear et al. 2001: 731).

Linked together, neurons form somewhat localized brain units, but "there are no single "centers" for vision, or language, or for that matter, reason or social behavior. There are "systems" made up of several interconnected brain units" (Damasio 2000: 15). While these distributed systems facilitate certain recognizable cognitive functions, the contribution of a given brain unit to the operation of the system hinges not only on the structure of the unit but also on its place in the system (Damasio 2000: 15). Sharp functional distinctions between regions in cortical processing do not exist (Bear et al. 2001: 648).

In neurological terms, when an object is perceived visually, there is a neural pattern (or mental image) that registers at various processing stages between the eye and the brain. Mental images need not be visual: auditory images, olfactory images, gustatory images, and somatosensory images all leave their marks on the system in one form or another (Damasio 1999: 318-319). As mentioned before, these images are not "contained" in single neurons or activated by solitary action potentials. They are formed through the firing of multiple action potentials across the system that more or less simultaneously stimulate specific combinations of neurons into "maps." Such mapping processes are crucial to the operation of complex brains. "Maps relate points on the two dimensional receptor sheets of the body (such as the skin or the retina of the eye) to corresponding points on the sheets making up the brain" (Edelman 1992: 19). Neurologist and neuroscientist Antonio Damasio notes that these mappings do not need to be point-for-point, utterly faithful facsimiles of the original perception; the brain constructs maps according to its own parameters (1999: 322), the only real constraint being that these parameters must be adaptive enough to succeed within their specific system (Edelman 1992: 204, 220).

These mappings are not found in a single location of the brain but are "distributed" over a number of locations (Damasio 2000: 106-107). Damasio describes how disparate aspects of a conceptualization of your Aunt Maggie might be distributed throughout the brain:

> There are dispositional representations for Aunt Maggie's voice in auditory association cortices, which can fire back to early auditory cortices and generate momentarily the approximate representation of Aunt Maggie's voice [...] Aunt Maggie as a complete person does not exist in one single site of your brain. She is distributed all over it, in the form of many dispositional representations, for this and that. (Damasio 2000: 102-103)

One great advantage of the human brain's distributed memory system is its relative immunity to catastrophic loss if some neurons die (Bear et al. 2001: 749). In fact, while neurons die every day, the loss of a single cell will not cause a person to forget the word "aardvark." The highly parallel and redundant nature of mental images assures that it is impossible for one neuron to contain the word or for a single neuron to allow access to it (Lamb 1998: 173). One disadvantage of the highly distributed memory system is relative instability of logic when compared to the precisely specified logical determinacy of systems such as Turing Machines (Edelman 1992: 225). Indeed, the reason that computers commonly exceed human capacities for chess and mathematical calculation is found in fundamental structural difference rather than memory capacity; the machines were designed to be rigorously logical and humans were not.

Neural control of bodily movement is facilitated by motor sequences, which are also mappings. These motor sequences are necessary for kicking a ball, playing the piano, or speaking. Motor sequences that are related to these tasks are "constructed or linked during consciously guided learning until a smooth, apparently effortless sensorimotor loop is executed speedily, reliably and unconsciously" (Edelman & Tononi 2000: 188). While motor sequences, including speech, are constructed using overt, conscious control, they are entrenched through repetition, eventually becoming global mappings for large-ly unconscious coordinated action.

In the case of sound perception, there is a certain amount of preprocess-ing that happens even before the sound image reaches Wernicke's area, one of the regions often associated with language comprehension. Intensity and fre-quency adjustments occur with the mechanical interaction of the tympanic mem-brane and the ossicles even before neural processing is initialized in the cochlea. Beginning with the cochlea, axons project stimulus toward the primary auditory cortex in an array called acoustic radiation (Bear et al. 2001: 355-372). The primary auditory cortex registers the incoming sound images on tonotopic maps (Bear et al. 2001: 380-381). These maps are probably composed of strips of neurons, called isofrequency bands, each band handling fairly similar char-acteristic frequencies. "In addition to the frequency tuning that occurs in most cells, some neurons are intensity tuned, giving a peak response to a particular sound intensity" (Bear et al. 2001: 381). Some neurons even key in on clicks, bursts of noise, frequency-modulated sounds and animal vocalizations.

With respect to linguistic communication, there is unanimity in assertions that "specialized language areas have evolved in the human brain that endow us with an incredibly flexible and creative system for communication" (Bear et al. 2001: 673). Deacon states, "[w]ithout question, children enter the world pre-disposed to learn human languages" (1997: 102), and cites neurobiological, anthropological, and clinical evidence to suggest that the brain has been "sig-nificantly overbuilt for learning symbolic associations" (1997: 413).

These observations notwithstanding, there is also agreement that lin-guistic processing should not be defined narrowly in terms of spoken language comprehension and production, but communication facility within a broad con-ceptual system. For instance, in some cases in which American Sign Language users are impaired in a way analogous to Broca's Aphasia, "the ability to move the hands is not impaired (i.e., the problem is not with motor control); rather, the deficit is specific to the use of hand movements for the expression of language" (Bear et al. 2001: 650). This demonstrates that linguistic communication is possible in the total absence of the sound images normally associated with linguistic processing, even though areas of the brain known to facilitate spoken language are in use. Such flexibility is built into the system by the ways that individual neurons act and interact: "Each brain is formed in such a way that its wiring and dynamics are enormously variable at the level of its synapses. It is a selectional system, and each brain is therefore unique" (Edelman & Tononi 2000: 213).

Activation and Entrenchment of Mappings within Conceptual Domains

Neuroscientist Donald Hebb proposed the existence of groups of simultaneously active neurons called "cell assemblies" that were connected to one another through reciprocal connections (Hebb 1949; cf. Bear et al. 2001: 522). According to this view, the representations of objects are held in short-term memory as long as corresponding activity reverberates through the cell assembly and if such reverberation continues long enough, the efficacy of the connections increases, resulting in memory consolidation. Another term for this selective strengthening of particular neural connections is "entrenchment." Importantly, while the medial temporal lobes (and the hippocampus, in particular) are thought to carry out key functions in the consolidation of declarative memories (Bear et al. 2001: 530), many of the cell assemblies that make long-term memory possible are not localized but are distributed across the neural system and likely incorporate "the same neurons that are involved in sensation and perception" (Bear et al. 2001: 522).

While it would be an overstatement to claim that the systems that facilitate perception and conception are one and the same (cf. Edelman 1992: 119), it is crucial to recognize that percepts and concepts have a great deal of overlap within the human neural system. Sensory perception necessarily begins, for example, with reception of sound by the cochlea in the ear and is then pre-processed for further transmission by the stereocilia and other front-line processing stages so crucial for interpreting auditory stimuli. Once beyond these sensory preprocessing stages, however, the neural differences between percepts and concepts may blur considerably.

Neuroscientist Edelman describes a "conceptual bootstrapping process" (1992: 119) in which all sensory modalities run in parallel, creating the complex scene we call consciousness. This complex scene is made possible by reentrant connections (combinations of feed-forward and feed-back connections) that correlate the conceptual categorizations already stored in memory and those perceptions experienced in real-time that are in the process of being categorized but which have not yet contributed lastingly to memory. In Edelman and Giulio Tononi's view, "concepts arise from the mapping by the brain itself of the activity of the brain's own areas and regions" (Edelman & Tononi 2000: 103). Practically, what this means is that, while different brain regions may be functionally (somewhat) distinct in their processes and the neural results of these processes, concepts emerge as narrow, single-modality mappings are interlinked to form a conceptual whole. The memory traces of past experiences, are mapped into the neural wiring. As experience-activated connectivity increases, the network of concepts will be constructed over time.

It should be no surprise to find that perceptions and conceptions are, if not two sides of the same coin, crucially related, because the world never offers exactly the same experience twice. Even for analogous experiences, small details will change from one perception to the next: same river, different water. Fortunately for humans, we remember objects, people, and places not by comparison with exact replicas of previous perceptions but by comparison with the abbreviated cognitive parameters stored in memory.

While perception and conception do have some overlap, remembered perception typically does not have the same force and immediacy of real-time present experience. This is accounted for by simply recognizing that conceptual activation (generally) does not feed back all the way into the front-line perception processing system which accounts for many of the most vivid sensory stimuli the brain will encounter. Of course there are a few unusual exceptions to this rule, one example being that of "otoacoustic emissions," the medical condition commonly called "ringing in the ears" (Bear et al. 2001: 367). Nevertheless, on the whole, perception seems more vivid than conception both because conception generally does not result in a significant level of feedback activation extending out to the apparatus of perception and because memories are stored partially according to internally useful parameters and so the entire image as originally sensed would not be available for recall in any case.

When new perceptions correspond roughly with previous perceptions stored in memory, the flurry of action potentials stimulated by the new perception will run through at least some of the same neural circuits activated by previous perceptions. This is (at least partially) how memory works: the traces of previous experiences of encounters with an aardvark are lit up when a new aardvark comes into view.

Each cascade of action potentials causes incremental changes as it spreads out through the neural system. Edelman and Tononi have remarked, "[i]f our view of memory is correct, in higher organisms every act of perception is, to some degree, an act of creation, and every act of memory is, to some degree, an act of imagination" (Edelman & Tononi 2000: 101). All perception results in neurobiological change of some sort and these incremental adjustments in the brain's "wetware" are, at least in the short term, irreversible. In selective systems such as the human brain, there is no "undo" function; the emergence of a pattern of activation occurs *ex post facto* (Edelman 1992: 168) and so the results of experience cannot be undone, only over-written.

See an aardvark once and the aardvark-related domain gets lit up. Every time an aardvark is perceived, a subset of the connections that link the entire

THE NEURAL FRAMEWORK   *23*

domain together get lit up again. With extensive exposure, one recognizes not only the appearance of an aardvark but the sound of an aardvark and the habits of an aardvark. If one is brave enough, perhaps even the feel of the fur. Before long, the "aardvark domain" becomes a well-worn set of paths through the mind (entrenched) and fleeting short-term memories solidify into stable long-term memories. The formerly vague aardvark-related conceptual domain has been solidified.

Now whether having such a clear understanding of aardvarks is useful or not is beside the point. That is to say, whether particular experiences that leave their mark in short term memory will ultimately prove adaptive or even useful for the individual organism is not an issue that the brain considers. Because neurons that "fire out of sync lose their link" (Bear et al. 2001: 731), newly formed associative connections that go unused thereafter will grow weaker over time and perhaps disappear altogether. In this way, the conceptual system comes to reflect the organism's environment. Nevertheless, whether strongly reinforced neural connections will actually prove adaptive and increase a given organism's chance of survival or not is anyone's guess.

In retrospect, it is evident that the general cognitive functions outlined in this chapter are a-cultural. While language, culture, and physical surroundings provide the inputs that build up the system during development, the system itself and the ways that it functions are stable from person to person. Our starting point for the analysis of literature, then, does not have anything to do with literature but with the nature of memory and attention. The neural network is equipped to do two important things: first, to activate the recollection of perceptions that have been stored in memory, and second, to create new conceptual domains and further develop existing conceptual domains within the associational system. These two aspects of cognition are not distinct but necessarily proceed in tandem, with far-reaching implications for literature and translation.

3

WORDS MAKING SENSE

The coherence among metaphors is a major source of the power of poetry. By forming a composition of several basic metaphors, a poet draws upon the grounding of those metaphors in common experience and knowledge. When that experience and knowledge cohere, the metaphors seem all the more natural and compelling.

George Lakoff & Mark Turner

(1989: 89)

The previous chapter gave an overview of how the neural system develops and how the instantiation and entrenchment of the products of perception result in the conceptual system. The chapter concluded with the observation that the neural network is equipped to do two important things: first, to activate recollections that have been stored in memory and, second, to create new conceptual domains and further develop existing domains within the associational system. This chapter will attempt to characterize some general ways in which the reading of a literary text affects the neural system of the reader. It should be kept in mind that, while these effects may be very small, they are irreversible.

Activation of Virtual Perceptions to Create Impressions

When literature is read, each word triggers a response in the conceptual system of the reader. Just as the sight of an aardvark will trigger a reaction in each part of the conceptual system related to the animal, the word "aardvark" does the

WORDS MAKING SENSE   *25*

same thing. What this means, in practical terms, is that language functions as a way for some outside agent to get another individual to "focus her attention on something" (Tomasello 1999: 97) and thereby direct the internal mental states of the perceiver toward some desired outcome. In fact, Tomasello goes so far as to assert that "linguistic symbols and constructions [are] nothing other than symbolic artifacts that a child's forebears have bequeathed to her" for the purpose of manipulating the attention of others (Tomasello 1999: 151).

Do all words have equal ability to leverage activity in the conceptual system? While every perceived word will leave its mark, apparently some words generate greater levels of activation than others. Insofar as "noticing" results in extra neural resources being allocated to a particular feature of perception, attention is a key sign of heightened neural activity. There are a number of features of words that lead to what linguists call "discourse prominence." Some of the features that have been reported to contribute to discourse prominence include recency (Lappin & Leass 1994), syntactic parallelism (Smyth 1994), and coherence relations (Kehler 2002). In that these and probably many other factors simultaneously influence the neural computation of the discourse prominence of any given linguistic item, the process is exceedingly complex.

Because the purpose of this chapter is to provide an overview of how the conceptual network of the reader is affected by reading at the whole discourse level, there will be no attempt to account for every possible factor that may leverage attention at the single-sentence level. Consequently this chapter will mention only a few general factors that, among literary scholars, are commonly acknowledged to leverage reader attention and give plausible if partial explanations of the cognitive processes behind these perceived literary categories. The specific factors that will be mentioned are "imagability," "novelty," and distinct "atmosphere."

Imagability and Memory Consolidation

Research by Freedman and Martin suggests that the imagability of a word is likely to be important for its instantiation into short-term memory (Freedman & Martin 2001: 221). This observation should come as no surprise to teachers of creative writing who are often quick to assert that it is better to "show" and not to tell. While imagability itself seems to be an extremely recurrent value, no two people will respond to images in exactly the same way. A broad range of individual differences depend on each individual's prior perceptions of images. For those who have never seen an aardvark, the word "aardvark" will be much less imagable than for those who have seen one on multiple occasions.

Of course, in the neural sense, imagability is not necessarily limited to vision. In that human minds store various sets of mapped parameters used for recognizing sounds, tastes, smells, and textures, it stands to reason that literary authors might use some of these other kinds of images to make their works more imagable, as well. Nevertheless, while there are some literary works that give extensive and extremely vivid descriptions of non-visual images (Natsume Sō-seki's short story "*Henna oto*" ("The strange sound"; Natsume 1911) comes to mind), a cursory glance through a typical novel will reveal that the primary mode of depiction used by most authors tends to be visual.

Sweetser notes that the human sense of vision allows us to locate and focus on specific objects among many and is a key element in the early category formation of children (Sweetser 1990: 38-39). Indeed, in ways comparable to the keen sense of smell of dogs or the keen hearing of bats, a great proportion of human cognitive resources seems to be allocated to facilitate vision. Bear et al. note that "about half of the cerebral cortex is involved in analyzing the visual world" (Bear et al. 2001: 281). Furthermore, certain aspects of relational memory and spatial understanding typically depend on visual stimuli to achieve maximal consolidation (Bear et al. 2001: 537-539).

Color and relative darkness or brightness are attributes that can be apprehended solely through vision. Textures, shapes, relative proportions, and configurations are also, if not exclusively, products of the visual senses, commonly perceived by way of vision. For this reason, the tendency for literary works to elicit visual aspects of perception should not be surprising.

Even the word "depiction" itself, having the idea of a "picture" as its root idea, connotes this visual primacy. This is not to say that having actual "vision" is necessary to appreciate these aspects of literature. People visually impaired from birth still have well-developed senses of texture, scale, proportion, and configuration; these have been developed entirely without the aid of vision. The human mind is remarkable in its flexibility. It should go without saying that literature written by and for the severely visually impaired, whether encoded in Braille or by way of spoken-word recordings, would not necessarily grant visually oriented depiction the pride of place afforded it in literature for those with sight. Even my working definition of literature as content communicated *visually* by way of printed words on a page will not always be useful, strictly speaking.

Already we find that broad trends in general cognitive function, in this case the relative dominance of vision among the senses in cognition, does not necessarily lead to any universal conclusion that literary aesthetics is primarily vision-oriented. The very fact that there are people without sight who appreciate literature creates the likelihood that visually-oriented "depiction," while highly prevalent, will not be the only viable mode of expression.

It should be mentioned here that poetry, which, at least traditionally, relies on the aural value of words to a greater extent than prose, does not replace visual emphasis with the aural sense, but rather complements the visual with the aural. Indeed, this idiosyncrasy lies at the very heart of many poets' discomfort with poetry in translation. (As this issue will be examined extensively in the following chapter, no attempt will be made to address it here.)

Preference for Novelty as the Cognitive By-product of Sensitization

One key aspect of literary style has always been "novelty," and indeed the "novel," which is now a relatively old literary form, once caused excitement precisely because it was a "new" genre. Martindale has offered psychological evidence that audiences become habituated to styles after a period of time and thereafter seek out newer styles (Martindale 1990). This tendency to become bored with the old and appreciate the new is easily corroborated by neurobiological findings with respect to individual organisms.

Sensitization occurs when a certain aspect of perception that normally might receive only scant attention is diminished or eliminated (Bear et al. 2001: 548). For example, after staying in a dark room for a long period of time, even a very dim light will evoke a strong response because the eye's receptors have adjusted to the dark conditions. In the same way, literary fashions change as readers become desensitized to longstanding literary features which subsequently reappear after the passage of time in some fresh, new form.

It is not ironic but entirely predictable that deemphasized literary features (the lack of attention to meter in early 21st century poetry comes to mind) create the necessary cognitive conditions that will likely cause meter to re-appear in some subsequent wave of literary fashion. At the level of the individual reader, a poet that has read nothing but late 20th century verse with its relative absence of strong auditory stimuli, would be more aware of (and possibly congenial to) aurally compelling poetry from preceding literary epochs.

Literature contains semantic novelty, as well. C.S. Lewis notes that fiction "tells about people that never really lived and events that never really took place" (Lewis 1967b: 266). In a sense, then, just as fresh styles cycle in and out of literary currency, character types and archetypes, settings, genres, and themes, as well, will appear either fresh or stale depending on the extent to which readers have become sensitized or habituated to them. Then again, the Internet has effectively splintered markets and readerships and so, as individuals seek novelty on their own terms and according to their own timing, lock-step literary fashion may be a thing of the past.

"Atmosphere" as the Complex Result of Differing Activation Patterns

It has been noted that literature relies heavily on visually oriented "depiction" in its descriptions. These "imagable" passages are helpful for making quick gains into short-term memory which is the initial prerequisite for consolidation into long-term memory. At the same time, literature is not simply a string of declarative facts and sets of activated perceptual parameters stored piecemeal in short- and long-term memory. The impressions created by a literary work may seem to be, but in fact are not, simply abstract or informative mental patterns.

Lewis noted how "[p]oetry most often communicates emotions, not directly, but by creating imaginatively the grounds for those emotions" (Lewis 1967a: 317). The basis for the emotional response elicited by literature lies firmly in a person's conceptual domains and conceptual association necessarily implies connection to the body's automatic emotional responses. These responses are just as much a part of the conceptual system as vision or audition (cf. Kutas 2006: 304; Maalej 2006).

In Murakami Haruki's novel, *Kafka on the Shore* (2005), when the extraterrestrial character Jack Daniels demonstrates his lack of concern for what he considers to be trivial human morality by tearing the hearts out of live cats before the eyes of a mortified human protagonist (Murakami 2005: 144-149), the reader probably does not experience the scene as an intellectually arid example of moral nihilism, but as a viscerally disturbing complex scene resulting in immediate dislike for the inhumane character. Authors will often use just such imaginatively crafted situations to manipulate emotional responses by way of conceptual input.

Whether offering excitement, sadness, or tension, an effective literary work will cause a reader to actively recall or at least passively reference analogous experiences from that person's individual past. By reading a narrative, the author uses premeditated combinations of characters, settings, and events to summon authentic memories of past experience within the mind of the individual reader. The permutations of depictable atmosphere are potentially infinite in variety and they vary subtly or completely from author to author, work to work, and reader to reader. When readers decide that they like "magical realism" and dislike "detective stories," they are only paring down and verbalizing the vague, extremely complex responses that the atmospheres of such works have elicited from their conceptual systems.

The flurry of action potentials triggered by words in the text race in unpredictable ways through the brain of the reader leaving a unique and unrepeatable impression. The impression will be unique because neural connections involve not single neurons but neuron populations (Edelman 1992: 73) and so there is a statistical element involved in patterns of spreading activation (Edelman 1992: 104). Even when exposure to the same set of written stimuli is repeated, the way in which an activation pattern fans out will be different from one occasion to the next. Furthermore, every time a neuron fires, there is resource depletion. For this reason, a given neuron, once activated, may not be available again until it has been electro-chemically "recharged," meaning that from one reading to the next it is a statistical certainty that some different neurons will be involved. While the impressions given by a particular text may be similar from reading to reading, there will be subtle differences and so, both because of minute random effects intrinsic to the neural system and because the reader's brain is subtly changing at all times, the impressions left by the reading of a text on a single occasion are unrepeatable.

As readers find pleasure or excitement or some other type of hoped for stimulus in the varied contexts of a literary work, they are motivated to keep reading and, if they have found value in it, to seek out similar virtual contexts in other works of the same genre or by the same author. These motivations for seeking out and reading certain types of literature may, in one sense, be considered epicurean. With respect to the atmosphere of a work, literature may be valued emotionally for the feelings it summons up. It is with this idea in mind that Kennedy and Gioia, in the preface to their introductory literature anthology, remark that literary appreciation begins with "delighted attention to words on a page" (Kennedy & Gioia 2002: xli).

As has been mentioned, though, atmospheres found in literature do not always result in feelings of delight. Sometimes feelings evoked may be negative. Sometimes feelings may be vague or emotionally complex. What we find then, is that the word "epicurean" is too limited in its traditional sense. At times the reader may be consciously delighted but motivations for reading will not always be straightforward or readily apparent. Suffice to say that we read because our neural systems encourage us to do so, whether the text read will finally result in positive feelings or psychological discomfort. Whatever the case, literature will continue to offer various complex conceptual atmospheres that can overcome the boredom of readers who have read too much of the same thing.

Integration of Preexisting Conceptual Domains

From an evolutionary perspective, is being able to understand literature broadly "adaptive" or simply an incidental by-product of sexual competition? Although those who study literature for a living may consider repulsive the very idea of literature having no more value than the tail-feathers of a peacock, evolutionary psychologists (e.g. Pinker 2002: 406) have asserted as much. Because this viewpoint characterizes literature as a superficial cultural epiphenomenon, the historical appraisal that literature is of intellectual value, an appraisal made by multiple generations of literary scholars and students, is being challenged.

There is a case to be made that literature offers cognitive benefits that may be considered adaptive in the broader sense. Associational activity is tied irretrievably to the mind's concepts and the integrated use of these is prerequisite for the skillful response to subjectively perceived reality and particularly for navigation of the extremely complex social environment that humans inhabit. As Tomasello puts it, "[h]umans have evolved in such a way that their normal cognitive ontogeny depends on a certain kind of cultural environment for its realization" (1999: 215). Tomasello further claims that this specific environment is characterized by linguistic symbols, constructions, and discourse patterns. Literature specializes in just such symbols, constructions, and discourse patterns. While literature is not the only aspect of human culture that can facilitate Tomasello's evolutionary "ratchet effect" (Tomasello 1999: 143-153), to deny that literature might serve such a purpose (and do so at a high level) out of hand is to deny that the quality of environmental stimuli contributes to the nature of subsequent learning and development.

Specifically, literature's cognitive value can be asserted in two different ways. First, it is possible to simply note the adaptive differences between "innocence" and "experience" (to quote two of Blake's poems). While "The Tyger" (Blake 1789: 8) burns bright and lives fiercely as a predator, "The Lamb" (Blake 1794: 42) is seen as helpless and likely to fall prey to the Tyger. Blake's anthropomorphized animals ("The Lamb" from Blake's collection *Songs of Innocence* and "The Tyger" from his *Songs of Experience*) are metaphorical examples which illustrate that while innocence and inexperience may be advantageous in a few limited situations, the very idea of education presupposes that having more experience, even vicarious experience, is more adaptive than having less.

Lewis characterized the power of poetic language as follows:

[It conveys] to us the quality of experiences which we have not had, or perhaps can never have, to use factors within our experience so that they become pointers to something outside of our experience — as two or more roads on a map show us where a town that is off the map must lie. (Lewis 1967b: 266)

Of course, judgments as to which kind of experiences or learning will be most helpful for learners represent crucial decisions. Some types of education and some types of literature may be irrelevant or disorienting. Overall, however, literature has the potential to provide the reader with a broad range of virtual experiences, stimulating previously undeveloped aspects of the associational system and thereby strengthening the reader's ability to sense and adapt to changes in the local social and relational environment.

Research by Blasko and Connine has shown that previous experience of a metaphor contributes to the rapid processing of that metaphor when encountered on subsequent occasions (Blasko & Connine 1993). To the extent that understanding metaphors is useful in everyday communication (and research has shown that they are very common (Gibbs 1994: 120) although commonly undetected) then previous experiences with metaphor in literature will be valuable for communication purposes. Not only does literature offer communicative content, it does so in a compact and easily accessible way. In fact, because literature is comprised of language and exposure to language increases one's ability to understand language and communicate in language, exposure to literature will offer cognitive benefits insofar as it provides linguistic content that helps the individual to hone communication skills difficult to develop by other means.

But wouldn't exposure to any kind of language accomplish the same purpose? To a certain extent, yes, but literature (at least potentially) offers a level of complexity not generally present in everyday discourse. As children develop their language skills they begin with relatively simple utterances and gradually increase the complexity of their discourse so as to achieve increasingly subtle communication goals (cf. Clark 1973: 586-594). For example, young children initially tend to mention events that occur around them in terms of the simple chronological order of occurrence rather than in terms of more complex relationships like cause-effect relationships (Clark 1973: 586). As they sense a need to express more sophisticated ideas, the complexity of the grammatical expressions they use increases concurrently. This correlation is assumed to result from the progressive development of young children's memory spans and linguistic knowledge (Clark 1973: 593). Tomasello's key point is that such cognitive abilities do not build out naturally irrespective of outside input but always develop in response to stimuli found in the environment. Literature is one set of stimuli that can stimulate various cognitive abilities.

Tomasello and Call have asserted that, of all species, only humans are capable of comprehending and creating extended narrative (Tomasello & Call 1997: 412). Language-related skills undoubtedly facilitate the understanding of extended narratives both for reasons of memory, strengthened in real time through language use, and corresponding habits of attention. The short attention spans of children determine that books read to young children will only be a few pages long with pictures, while a novel for cognitively developed adults will often feature more than 400 pages of densely packed text. Of course, not many adults will have the attention span or free time necessary to read such a novel in one sitting but nevertheless, the cognitive skills necessary to finish a long novel, even over a period of days or weeks, do not develop spontaneously. The ability to understand long, complex narratives requires a steady increase in skill level over a long apprenticeship. Extensive, focused reading (as has traditionally been a component of higher education) hones the narrative comprehension abilities and analytical skills that make such reading productive. Without the apprenticeship, the words on the page of a long and difficult text may be read and individually understood, but the work as a whole won't make sense.

Connectivity within and between Conceptual Domains

In literature generally, various domains of experience (it will be useful to term these conceptual domains) interact and create fresh ideas and novel atmospheres within the mind of the reader. The succession of domain activations stimulated by a literary text is primarily accomplished by the strategic sequencing of words.

Ultimately, if words are artificial handles that attach themselves to clumsy, bulky concepts for ease in manipulation, literature and other extended speech sequence performances allow us not only to perceive concepts in succession creating unique moods and atmospheres, but to juggle them and make them interact with predictable and unpredictable semantic consequences (cf. Tomasello & Call 1997: 408). Every perception of a word on a page accomplishes some microscopic, incremental change in the mind of the reader; for this reason, every time complex patterns of words are perceived in literary context, new ideas and new patterns of integration result in the mind.

While a poorly orchestrated text will yield relatively unpredictable neural effects, a skillfully orchestrated text will maneuver the mind of the reader through a series of images, scenes, and events that, in some cases, has been designed by the author to lead the reader to a final predetermined conceptual outcome. Readers differ and so precise outcomes also differ, but the very fact that communication occurs at all owes to the relative similarities between the concepts of the reader and the concepts of the author, two individuals with different but (perhaps) somewhat analogous experience sets.

It is not enough, however, to simply mention fleeting impressions and the subtle changes in conceptualization that remain after language has "done its thing" as if language served no other purpose than to create arbitrary impressions. Lewis made the assertion that "language is by no means merely an expression, nor a stimulant, of emotion, but a real medium of information. Which information, may, like any other, be true or false" (Lewis 1967b: 266). From a cognitive perspective, this observation must be clarified. In that language is utterly dependent upon the neural system in which it has developed to ascertain "actionable" information from the viewpoint of the individual, judgments as to truth or falsehood are inevitably made with respect to this viewpoint (cf. Lakoff & Johnson 1980: 180). Language offers not truth, but information that may be deemed true from a certain embodied perspective. To the extent that many individuals share the same (or similar) perspectives, estimations of truth tend to correspond.

How does the mind interpret "truth"? There are two recurrent cognitive strategies that support the distinctively human way in which language-users negotiate truth in the world around them. Although these strategies have linguistic aspects, they are not primarily linguistic in nature but rather conceptual. Metonymy and metaphor are conceptual phenomena that play crucial roles in helping humans make sense of the world around them.

Metonymy may be understood as a direct outcome of the neural rule of thumb, "what fires together, wires together." Concepts are formed as varying modes of perceptual experience co-occur and thereby wire themselves together into a coherent set of interrelated neural dispositions. The sound, smell, and appearance of an aardvark will each leave memory traces in the perceiver's mind simultaneously when an aardvark is present. Co-occurrence leads to correlation. This strategy is nothing other than the logical fallacy "guilty by association." If it smells like an aardvark, sounds like an aardvark, and looks like an aardvark, it must be an aardvark. As such, metonymy is the linguistic expression of a very basic cognitive strategy not unique to humans, a strategy that forms the basis for conceptualization in all sentient creatures. Humans are simply the only creatures that can lexicalize the conceptual connections.

Of course, sometimes co-occurrence is a matter of random contiguity. If a police officer is spotted at a post office once, the fact will be noticed but will not immediately bind the two concepts together. Only repeated correlation will cause the "guilty by association" effect to kick in and gradually connect the previously separate concepts, "police officer" and "post office" within the mind of the perceiver.

When a text states that "the police officer walked into the post office" the statement does not necessarily imply any demonstrable correlation between the police officer and the post office. They are logically unrelated but, in the context of the narrative, they happen to occupy the same scene. In literature, the author has the ability to combine unrelated conceptual domains by manipulating the contiguity relations of the words in the text. No relationship between the two conceptual domains has been posited. The text depicts an apparently random juxtaposition of elements.

In real life, some ideas are naturally connected to other ideas, so much so that from a certain viewpoint, they necessarily seem to be part of the same conceptual domain. The image of a postage stamp, although simply a piece of perforated, colored paper with adhesive on the back, may stand in for the entire postal system because the two are closely related in a particular conceptual domain of experience. Post offices, stamps, mail trucks, and postal worker uniforms are all part of the conceptual package we call the "postal system." The conventional and organically occurring links between these concepts have been developed through the consistent co-occurrence of constituent elements. A child will not understand the postal system in its totality. Nevertheless, the child does know what a stamp is, at least as a kind of colorful sticker. Only gradually, as the connections and relationships between the disparate elements are understood, does the child develop the "postal system" concept in which all of the elements become connected. These elements in the single conceptual domain are bound together organically by the cognitive function that (in the realm of language) motivates metonymy.

Of course, the postal system is not the only conceptual domain in which a post office is an element. The post office is a government-sanctioned institution. Because the police officer is a government-sanctioned official, there is an umbrella concept that covers both, namely the idea of "public service." Similar to gestalts in visual perception, the shape of concepts summoned to mind by a particular element in perception may flip back and forth depending on which aspect of that element one is attending to. Viewing a stamp, one might understand the postal service in terms of mail delivery but viewing the flag at the front

of the building might rather cause one to remember the public nature of the institution. Just as words do not simply adhere as "labels" to concepts in a "one-to-
one correspondence" fashion (Lakoff 1987: 333), varying conceptualizations
will overlap in the specific cognitive activation patterns they are tied into. For
this reason, one's view of a concept can change subtly as one's point of reference changes.

While metonymic connections bind together the disparate elements of a
single conceptual domain, metaphoric connectivity links up specific aspects of
otherwise unrelated conceptual domains. Example 3.1 will illustrate this point:

Example 3.1

Sending a letter at the post office is like asking a child to get dressed by herself.

When I observe that sending a letter by regular mail at the post office is like asking a child get dressed without help, I juxtapose two otherwise unrelated domains
of experience with the expectation that the reader will be able to intuitively locate
the main point of the analogy. The two concepts are artificially linked by contiguity in the linguistic utterance or text and a metaphor is created. Simply by
lexicalizing this metaphor, the two unrelated conceptual domains will be activated in the mind of the reader and both distinct parts of the network will "light
up."

Attention is leveraged when the part of the neural system which is receiving action potentials from both domains begin to fire at a higher rate than the
surrounding parts. We notice things precisely because there has been some
upsurge in neural activity somewhere in our subconscious. As this upsurge
occurs, the subconscious neural activity, outside of our awareness and beyond
our conscious control, spikes and spreads activation beyond the associational part
of the brain and feeds out to activate cell assemblies in the perceptual parts of
the brain. We become aware of non-perceptual activity only as that activity

swells up from the subconscious and breaks the surface of perception in some modality.

What if there is no common element in the two conceptual domains that have been lexically linked together and purported to be a metaphor? Then, for that perceiver, there is no metaphor there. The link between the two conceptual domains remains to be established. There is no connection. At least from the point of view of the perceiver in question, it is an inapt metaphor which yields no added cognitive value. Now there are a number of reasons why this might happen. Perhaps the originator of the metaphor did not choose domains well. Perhaps the perceiver of the purported metaphorical statement did not have sufficiently developed conceptual domains to reveal the common elements.

The reason that children often do not understand metaphor is not because the processes that enable metaphor are not yet functioning. They are functioning. The problem is that the limited nature of their experiences has not allowed enough time for their conceptual domains to be filled out.

When conceptual domains are not fully informed by experience, all but the mot basic metaphors will fall flat. This viewpoint receives confirmation in brain studies using ERPs (Event-related Brain Potentials), which have shown that "college students with lower verbal IQ, which is correlated with working memory, showed no automatic activation of [metaphor], but older people, regardless of IQ, did show metaphor activation" (Blasko & Kazmerski 2006: 281).

When metaphor succeeds however, some conceptual element that is common to both conceptual domains will become relatively more active than those surrounding it. This will happen because action potentials are cascading to it from the connections that comprise not one but two conceptual domains. The relatively greater number of incoming action potentials pushes the neuron cell assembly's activity level over a critical threshold and the neural element common to both metaphorical domains lights up.

As the critical threshold is passed, the particular neurons that have been disproportionately activated send electrochemical signals to the other neural modalities of that element. In the case of the simile previously stated in Example 3.1, namely that "receiving a letter said to have been sent by regular mail at the post office is like asking a child to get dressed without parental supervision," one commonality is the necessity to allow time for completion of the assigned task. Perhaps the word "waiting" will be activated in the phonological repository of words related to the concept "waiting." Perhaps the understanding of the metaphor will be intuitive and mostly subconscious and so the perceiver will find it difficult to lexicalize the nature of the newfound understanding.

Ultimately, whether the common element in the metaphor expressed above will be noticed or not depends on two things: how much time the individual has spent waiting for mail to arrive and how much time the individual has spent waiting for children to get dressed without adult assistance. If either of these conceptual domains is insufficiently filled out with respect to the relevant aspect, the metaphor will likely fail. Individual differences in personal experience will determine the aptness of that metaphor for a given person.

In a sufficiently intuitive metaphor (and good metaphors are often good precisely because they are intuitive), this process will be almost instantaneous and will result in a clearly understood knowledge of the correlation which can immediately be explained in words. These metaphors, precisely because they result in effective communication so quickly, are likely to become fossilized into colloquialisms that then proceed down the road to eventually becoming dead metaphors. Less intuitive metaphors will take more time and result in less clearly understood relationships between the two domains. Novel metaphors that have limited correlation between conceptual elements or involve unusual conceptual domains may never be understood except by a limited number of people and will probably not catch on and become conventionalized.

Compelling metaphors are compelling precisely because they are memorable and access stable connections that tend not to differ from individual to individual. Unconvincing metaphors fail not because they are not metaphors but because the link between the domains is not basic enough to result in a neural activity spike in the minds of most people.

If a particular metaphor is only encountered once and thereafter goes unused, the neural connections that comprise it may in fact wither and effectively disappear. Through consistent use, however, the metaphor will become a thoroughly integrated part of the semantic system (cf. Edelman 1992: 104). If we chant the mantra "life is a journey" often enough, soon we may not be able to see life in terms of anything but a journey. The neurally entrenched metaphor will have become a cognitive rut that is difficult to break free from.

Schäffner has noted that much translation-related research extant has viewed metaphor as "a linguistic expression which is substituted for another expression (with a literal meaning), and whose main function is stylistic embellishment of the text" (2004: 1254). Just as cognitive linguistics research on embodiment has undermined the idea of literal meaning in its strict theoretical sense (e.g. Lakoff & Turner 1989 : 110), Conceptual Metaphor Theory has shown that metaphor is not simply a mode of rhetorical artifice but actually a crucial conceptual phenomenon without which human linguistic communication would be extremely inflexible at best.

Extended and Diffused Forms of Metaphor

The examples of metaphor often mentioned by cognitive linguists (e.g. LIFE IS A JOURNEY) are typically metaphors that offer compact and readily analyzable lexical profiles, a prime example being idiomatic expressions (e.g. Lakoff & Johnson 1980; Gibbs 1994: 307-309). In such examples, the necessary information for understanding the metaphor tends to be found within a single short sentence. It makes sense that this kind of compact metaphor has been highlighted by linguists and experimental psychologists; cognitive linguists and psychologists are trained to pare down their subject to optimize experimentation and analysis. Studies that include analysis of extended metaphor have been done but this research too has been constrained by analytical and pedagogical necessities. Too many factors will easily cloud analysis and complicate explanation and so, even for research on "extended" metaphor, the verdict seems to be "the less extended the better." Metaphors neatly packaged in compact linguistic settings are ideal both as analytical and explanatory commodities.

Due to the experimental and analytical problems associated with forms of metaphor that display a less than clearly demarcated lexical profile, extended forms of metaphor have been neglected. It is ironic that the Conceptual Theory of Metaphor, which repeatedly asserts that metaphor is not a linguistic but a conceptual phenomenon, inevitably packages explanations of conceptual metaphor as if it were a completely linguistic phenomenon. Diffused-domain metaphor (which has also been called "megametaphor"), in which metaphor functions despite maintaining a low linguistic profile, has been all but ignored as a subject of both theoretical and empirical investigation, some exceptions being papers by Werth (1994), Stockwell (2002), Kimmel (2005), and previous papers by the author of this book (Strack 2000; 2004; 2006a; and 2006b).

Extended metaphor (sometimes called "sustained metaphor") occurs when multiple entailments of a single metaphor are present within a discourse. These entailments typically reflect intuitively evident correspondences between the two conceptual domains. Both the metaphor and its entailments are detectable at the sentence or multiple sentence level. This rather common type of metaphorical extrapolation is epitomized by the explanation commonly given for the LIFE IS A JOURNEY metaphor. When we extend the metaphor LIFE IS A JOURNEY, we understand one's birth as the beginning of the journey, one's death as the end of the journey, and the events of one's life as the path along which a person travels.

The idea of extended metaphor alone is not sufficient to explain the subtle ways in which metaphors function in literature (and in other forms of non-literary discourse, as well). According to Werth, "megametaphors" (1994: 97) are "overarching" metaphors that express the "undercurrent" or "gist" of an extended discourse. Diffused-domain metaphor in extended discourse is often difficult to detect and confirm because it tends to function surreptitiously by way of scattered references rather than overtly through verbally compact comparisons. Stockwell characterizes megametaphor as the situation that occurs when "conceptual metaphors occur repeatedly throughout a text, often at pivotal moments and often in the form of thematically significant extended metaphors" (Stockwell 2002: 111). In a previous paper, I have noted that "[m]egametaphors represent a specific type of extended metaphor in which fragments of each metaphorical domain are instantiated within a text cumulatively while overt connections between the source and target domains prove elusive if not altogether absent" (Strack 2006a: 38).

In this book, I have chosen to use the term "diffused-domain metaphor" because I feel it expresses the nature of the metaphor better than the terms used previously. This type of extended metaphor is not necessarily "big" as implied by the name megametaphor. "Diffused-domain metaphor" is a more accurate term because it describes the way the domain elements are spread out through the text. As such, diffused-domain metaphors give literary authors access to an extremely subtle form of metaphor that tends to function outside of the reader's conscious awareness.

This type of metaphor is not new. Literary critic Booth has observed that authors tend to avoid direct commentary concerning the meanings they hope to elicit because overtly didactic comments by the narrator can seem obtrusive. He remarks:

Knowing this danger, novelists very early developed methods for disguising their portents as part of the represented object. Long before the dogmas

about showing rather than telling became fashionable, authors often con-
cealed their commentary by dramatizing it as scenery or symbol. (Booth
1961: 196)

While short on linguistic analysis of the phenomenon, Booth's observation clearly points both to conscious authorial use of diffused-domain metaphor and critical awareness that it has been commonly used.

How can we explain the function of extended metaphor and diffused-
domain metaphor in neural terms? With respect to polysemy, Cutler and Clifton
have noted that "[s]tudies of the cross-modal priming task have produced evidence for momentary simultaneous activation of all senses of an ambiguous
word, irrespective of relative frequency or contextual probability" (Cutler &
Clifton 1999: 140). There is no reason to believe that neural activation of the connections which instantiate metaphor should work in a different manner.
Reference to any element in an extended metaphor, particularly if that metaphor
is already entrenched, will lead to widespread if momentary neural activation
among the rest of the constituent elements in the metaphor. In terms of
metaphor, then, when metaphorical elements are referred to in the course of
depiction, all entrenched metaphorical extensions relating to the domains in
question will be momentarily primed. Thereafter, specific details in the text that
coincide with any parts of the already primed constellation of metaphors will further activate elements of the metaphors that have already been stimulated by the
broad, indiscriminate momentary priming.

Now that the theoretical foundations have been laid out, it is time to give
a practical example of how diffused-domain metaphor functions in a literary text.
Nagai Kafū's short story "The Peony Garden" (Nagai 1909; Nagai 1972) is a
good example of how multiple types of extended metaphor can be surreptitiously
interwoven into a narrative. In the story, the narrator and a geisha named Koren
travel by boat to view a famous seasonal peony exhibition at a garden some dis-

tance down a canal that extends off of the Sumida River. As the pair travels along the canal, they reconsider their previous decision not to get married. In the end, the two decide that they already know each other too well and so marriage would hold no excitement for them. During the trip, they think back to decisions they have made and the river journey itself mirrors their psychological states. For example, along with their decision not to get married, they have also decided not to have children. Perhaps to accentuate this aspect of their relationship, the depiction notes on multiple occasions that the disembodied voices of children can be heard, apparently playing unseen somewhere in the vicinity. Finally they arrive and view the peonies:

Example 3.2

The peonies were already falling. Even the blossoms that had not lost all their petals were faded badly, their hearts black and gaping. Had they been exposed to bright sunlight and fresh breezes, they would have fallen by now. The weariness and boredom of having been made to bloom too long seemed to flow from each blossom. These peonies had something in common with us, I thought. (Nagai 1972: 53; Seidensticker Translation)

Disappointed, they return back down the river and as they make their way, the voices of unseen children become louder and louder.

There are two submerged metaphors in the story that combine to reflect the psychological states of the characters depicted. The river journey (including a trip up a canal of memory) itself corresponds to the long years that the two have spent together; their reflections during the boat trip are mirrored by events on the shore. As they are portrayed traveling along this fictional expression of the metaphor TIME IS A RIVER, the disembodied voices of the unseen children on the shore and the couple's discussion of their decision not to have children serve to very subtly point to a link between the journey the couple is taking and the years they have spent together.

The other metaphor, evident in the title of the work, links the psycho-logical states of the protagonists with the physical condition of the peony flow-ers on display. Just as the flowers are past peak, so the couple's relationship has faded. Following the logic of this HUMAN RELATIONSHIPS ARE PLANTS metaphor, the reader may infer that the couple's relationship will not likely last much longer.

Kafū has taken these two unrelated metaphors, TIME IS A RIVER and HUMAN RELATIONSHIPS ARE PLANTS, and surreptitiously diffused elements relating to each domain into the depiction of scenery and events in the narrative. No explicit interdomain link between the decision by the couple not to have chil-dren and the disembodied voices of children emanating from the shore is appar-ent at any point in the narrative although some indirect hints are evident in ret-rospect. The link between the couple's psychological state and the physical con-dition of the peonies, however, is overt (expressed through the narrator's simi-le in the final line of Example 3.2). Nevertheless, the entire extended metaphor will only be available to the reader subconsciously or in retrospect by way of conscious analysis.

The effects resulting from diffused-domain metaphor differ from other types of high-profile metaphor in that time to reflect upon the story may be required before the correlations between the domains are noticed. This is undoubtedly the case with respect to Kafū's short story, which, without the metaphors, would otherwise have been a rather unremarkable account of a cou-ple discussing their relationship troubles.

The linguist Roman Jakobson, in noting how symptoms of aphasia seem to gravitate toward one or the other of the "metaphoric and metonymic poles" (Jakobson 1956: 76), notes a parallel with various literary traditions, especially romanticism and realism. His assumption is that realist authors focus on metonymy and not metaphor. For example, he notes how, in *Anna Karenina,*

Tolstoy's depiction of Anna's suicide at the train station (Tolstoy 2000: 768) emphasizes, of all things, Anna's red handbag. While correctly identifying this "realistic" element of depiction as being strangely foregrounded, Jakobson has missed the forest for the tree. The synecdochic detail he mentions is indeed metonymic but it is simultaneously part of an unnoticed metaphor. The reference to the red bag seems only to be metonymic because its counterpart conceptual domain is totally absent from the scene and the interdomain link (by which the metaphor has already been created) is found much earlier in the story.

In fact, the same red handbag made a previous appearance as Anna settled herself in for a train journey (Tolstoy 2000: 99-100). In this same red bag, Anna keeps an English novel through which she has been experiencing life vicariously. As she reads the novel, she begins to resent the fact that her experiences are only vicarious and begins to long for the exhilaration she would no doubt feel if she were to strike up an affair with Vronsky. Now at the end of the story, just before Anna dives under another train to end her life, Tolstoy depicts the red bag again, a physical reminder of Anna's previous decision. The reappearance of the bag represents a second chance for Anna to forget her own misfortunes and look for joy vicariously in the joys of others. She is only able to throw herself under the train after she has thrown this red bag away.

The red handbag is important in the story not because it is so realistically depicted but as a concrete image that points directly to an abstract idea that Tolstoy was trying to bring to the reader's attention. Why did Tolstoy make the bag red? Because red attracts attention and he wanted the readers to notice it. By contrasting Anna's and Levin's lives in the story, Tolstoy is showing why "All happy families are alike" and "each unhappy family is unhappy in its own way" (Tolstoy 2000: 1). To the extent that family members (and especially parents) can forego their own dreams so as to support the dreams of others (the children), happy families remain happy. Unhappy families, in contrast, become unhappy as a result of any of a number of potentially destructive decisions made solely

48

for the benefit of the individual.

The "red bag" that Anna throws away is the concrete counterpart domain to the abstractly depicted domain of Levin's decision to link his own happiness to the happiness of others. The handbag is the metaphorical "keystone" that binds the two otherwise apparently unrelated characters, Levin and Anna, together. The two metaphorical planes coexist in Tolstoy's depiction precisely because they have been painstakingly constructed so as to form this diffused-domain metaphor. Jakobson assumes that Tolstoy's emphasis on the red bag in this crucial scene is metonymy for the sake of metonymy when in fact it is metonymy for the sake of undetected metaphor.

So once the author decides to co-opt everyday metaphor and metonymy for use in the literary realm, what can be done with them? Whatever the author wants to do with them. "Social conflict" among characters or a single character's "internal conflict" can be accentuated by the instantiation of a concrete metaphorical domain to mirror the abstract social or individual domain portrayed. If the relationship between "cause and effect" is viewed as a metonymic relationship between certain actions and commonly associated outcomes, "irony" is accomplished by defying metonymic understanding and depicting outcomes that apparently do not follow from their antecedents. Largely subconscious feelings of "tension" may be elicited in the reader by juxtaposing characters with differing metaphorical views of the world. Paradox can be instantiated by giving equal validity to mutually exclusive diffused-domain metaphors within the plot. Conceptual domains, metonymy, and metaphor, are nothing less than practical narrative equipment that skilled literary authors utilize to accomplish their conceptual heavy lifting.

But is it necessary to use these tools to create literature? Undoubtedly, some authors seek to avoid using such artifice. Very certainly, metaphor especially can be used in clumsy fashion and either fail to function properly or do so in too conspicuous a manner, thereby ruining the intended effect (cf. Booth 1961:

196). Still, metaphor is readily available because it is recurrent not only in everyday linguistic communication but in thought itself. For this reason, authors that attempt to avoid using metaphor will tend to do two things: first of all, they are likely to compensate for their lack of semantic artifice by exaggerating other literary aspects of their work. Secondly, they will use metaphor unconsciously anyway. Because metaphor functions primarily in the subconscious, everyday language users and authors alike are unlikely ever to realize the full extent of their dependency on it.

4

THE REASON FOR RHYME

The goal of poetic expression is not simply found in expressing sentimental content for the sake of sentimentality. Neither is it found in imaginative
depiction for the sake of imagination. Moreover it should not be seen as one
more form of ideological propaganda. The real goal of poetry is, by way of
such measures, to probe the essence of emotion found in the innermost
human heart and thereby cause those emotions to well up.

Poetry pinches the *nerves of emotion*. It is a *living, functioning psychology.*

Hagiwara Sakutarō

(1917a: 10; Strack Translation)

In chapter 3, I characterized two general results of associative activity in the
brain. These were, first, the activation of mappings that store traces of previous
experiences to allow for recognition and response, and second, the further development of preexisting conceptual domains. Within this context, it was noted that
particularly "imagable" words may be used by an author to increase the likelihood of instantiation of some aspect of the text into short-term memory. This
particular feature evident in the human neural system demonstrates the power
attention has over the system as a whole. If an author can manage to leverage
the attention of the reader, the reader's neural resources will be at the author's
disposal, at least momentarily. In this chapter, I will examine a few more aspects

THE REASON FOR RHYME   *51*

of "attention" and "noticing" and look carefully at the ways in which they interface with the cultural categories of literature.

Are Aesthetics simply Personal Preferences Writ Large?

In much discussion of aesthetics, it seems to be taken for granted that aesthetic
preferences, because they seem to vary at the level of culture, must therefore
result from trends among the personal preferences of those belonging to a given
cultural group. They are seen to be differences in "personal taste" realized in
aggregate. In the previous chapter, though, I mentioned the "imagability" of
words as an aspect of language that functions as a basic aspect of cognition.

Is it possible that a reader's response to a word's imagability may simply be due to the fact that the reader has had certain individual experiences and
has undergone a cultural apprenticeship that has led her to value imagability?
Isn't it possible that imagability might be downplayed in a given aesthetic value
system? This depends on how much the system that processes visual imagery is
able to adapt to the cultural setting the individual inhabits and also on how much
individuals are able to intentionally ignore basic aspects of cognition when it
suits their purposes to do so.

With respect to vision, the perception of color is "largely determined by
cones in the retina and subsequent cortical processing" which, except for those
people who are color blind, means that "color isn't arbitrary" (Feldman 2006:
103-104). If the visual system is working, it works mostly in the same way even
in different people. On the other hand, Kay and Kempton (1984) have shown that
when a language has a word for "blue-green" that another language does not,
speakers of the first language are more easily able to recognize the color and differentiate it from other colors than speakers of the second language.

The origin of the Japanese expression, "*Jūnin tōiro*" （十人十色 ; "ten
people, ten colors"), lies in the fact that, although people tend to process the perception of color similarly, personal preferences nevertheless differ. So while the

initial stages of perception processing are relatively stable from person to person, our responses to the post-processing results of such perceptions are apt to be influenced by culture and personal experiences.

As a metaphor, we might distinguish between a computer's factory-programmed preset parameters and the "user options" adjusted gradually by an individual computer user over a long period of time. The cognitive presets will be a strong motivating factor behind whatever appears to be extremely recurrent in aesthetic awareness. Conversely, the gradually accreted preferences account for differences in aesthetic value from person to person and culture to culture.

The primary goal of this chapter will be to probe the interface between cultural concepts and the "hardware" of aesthetic awareness by examining how individuals view the categories that comprise literature. How do the basic elements of human cognition interact with cultural factors to result in the aesthetic differences we commonly perceive? To what extent may they become adapted to individual and cultural tastes? Before proceeding, however, it will be necessary to mention a question (frequently asked) that will not lead to useful answers about literature in its broadest and most universal sense.

Irrelevant Question: What is the definition of literature?

Many introductory literature textbooks begin by giving a number of conflicting definitions of literature followed by a comment to the effect that literature really has no stable definition and so if something seems like literature to you, then that's literature. I have typically offered such an array of definitions and the same final assessment in my own *Introduction to Comparative Literature* course. Such an anti-definition perfectly matches the multicultural age in which we live and, in fact from a cognitive linguistics viewpoint, is a realistic way to handle the question.

And yet inflexible definitions are somehow comforting. Inevitably, quite soon after I offer students this heterogeneous collection of conflicting and even

THE REASON FOR RHYME   *53*

mutually exclusive definitions of literature, I begin to analyze and categorize these definitions. I say something like:

> Ultimately, each new definition tends to fall into one of two general categories: the pragmatic or the epicurean. On the one hand, literature may be valued as a practical tool that leads to something else, be it spiritual enlightenment, worldly wisdom, social power, or the illusion of possessing these. On the other hand, literature can be "good" in and of itself. It is pleasant to read literature. It is an entertaining pastime. It offers vicarious experiences. It stimulates the mind and this in itself is enjoyable. Those who choose to defend literature will either do so because it is good in itself or leads to something good. In fact, though, literature is often defended for both reasons.

Only later do I reflect back on what I have said. Characterizing literature in terms of the epicurean and the pragmatic seems to be nothing more than a recapitulation of Samuel Johnson's adage, "Poetry is the art of uniting pleasure with truth" (Johnson 1781: 57). While such a formulation has intuitive appeal, does this nifty dichotomy reflect the nature of literature or the nature of my desire to understand things in terms of nifty dichotomies?

The history of literary criticism is littered with nifty dichotomies. Tabakowska notes how Polish linguistics scholars were preoccupied with splitting linguistic analysis of texts into "grammatical" and "stylistic" components (Tabakowska 1993: 11). Author Henry James tops Johnson and the linguists by offering up not just one but three dichotomies, or is it three-in-one? James felt that no elements of literature are purely rhetorical because, in literature, "substance and form, subject and treatment, matter and manner become fused" (Booth 1961: 104).

If one fuses these various dichotomies together, some central issues relating to literature begin to emerge: one general "pragmatic pole" seems to encompass concepts like "the grammatical," substance, subject, matter, and truth, while the other seemingly opposite "epicurean pole" characterizes literature in terms of style, form, treatment, manner, and pleasure. While the term "grammatical" seems not to be an exact fit, in general there is a kind of coherence. Is there any evidence to support the existence of such a schism? Yes, but the schism is not in literature itself but in the way the mind perceives it, that is, in the way human cognition is wired so as to understand things in terms of dichotomies, parallelisms, and metaphors.

In Regier's connectionist modeling, it is an intriguing finding that "learning concepts together as a set was critical for the purpose of learning without explicit negative evidence" (Regier 1996: 132) and that concepts learned in isolation take more time to converge on correct answers than those that are learned as a pair (Regier 1996: 140). Although connectionist modeling itself does not confirm anything about the human brain, the fact that network models display features that show parallel activation to be an aid to understanding hints that the human semantic network could work according to such a principle, as well. Such a viewpoint is entirely consistent with the idea that parallelism is an artistic artifice precisely because of its neural efficacy.

On the Linearity of Literature and Parallel Cognition

Northrop Frye has observed "that information is not a placid river of self-explanatory facts: it comes to us prepackaged in ideological containers, and many of these containers have been constructed by professional liars" (Frye 1990: 118). This statement is noteworthy for two reasons. First, because Frye points out that there is no single correct way to put an idea into language. Second, the statement is noteworthy for the metaphors he uses to characterize communication: a river and containers. The first metaphor is linear, likening the way language is expressed temporally to the flow of a river. The second metaphor, containers, implies the "outward form" and "inner content" dichotomy just mentioned.

The relationship between "time" as we know it in moment-to-moment experience and "time" as it is expressed in literature is a highly abstracted one. Authors cannot express anything in language without making a choice concerning how time will be expressed. While some authors undoubtedly express temporality according to convention without giving it much thought, others consciously explore the implications of the problem. Author Raymond Chandler was indirectly hinting at one of the ways in which authors manipulate time in narrative when he remarked: "A good story cannot be devised; it has to be distilled" (Chandler 1997: 75). For an author to "distill" a story, the unnecessary, nonessential elements must be elided in the editing process. Lodge is thinking along similar lines when he explains that "[t]ime must be foreshortened to achieve intensity, but in foreshortening the novelist must use *dissimulation* successfully in order to preserve the illusion of reality" (Lodge 1977: 44).

The problem is that real-time experience for the individual proceeds in multiple perceptual modalities simultaneously while the author can (for the most part) express only one modality at a time due to the linear nature of reading words of text on a printed page. This is no less true for speech, although gestures and other communicative content may supplement modalities not present in the lexical items alone. What are the aspects of cognition that can account for the fact that we can make sense of such linear communication?

It is a basic tenet of neurobiology that "neurons that fire together, wire together." Bear, Connors, and Paradiso explain this process in the following way:

> Imagine a hippocampal neuron receiving synaptic inputs from three sources, A, B, and C. Initially, no single neuron input is strong enough to evoke an action potential in the postsynaptic neuron. Now imagine that inputs A and B repeatedly fire at the same time. Because of spatial summation, inputs A and B are now capable of firing the postsynaptic neuron and causing [long-

term potentiation]. Only the active synapses are potentiated, and these, of course, are the synapses belonging to inputs A and B. (Bear et al. 2001: 792-793)

What we notice here is that repeated simultaneous activation between different parts of the neural network results in increasing correspondence of neural activity. This being the case, when a great number of elements of the neural system are activated simultaneously, a broad and general activation will occur creating relatively diffused connections. Conversely, when the elements or modalities activated are limited, the interconnection between them will be stronger, creating more delimited and therefore stronger connections. This is exactly the kind of picture that Regier's connectionist model points to.

In a text, the repeated juxtaposition of two elements within a short time-frame, whatever they happen to be, will increase the mutual activation of those conceptual elements in the mind, thereby resulting in connections between the two. Undoubtedly, grammar-cued subroutines play a part in this complex process. Nevertheless, some words have a stronger effect on the system than others, with imagability being one factor that leads to instantiation in short-term memory. As a result, when particularly imagable words are used, the corresponding spreading activation between the two concepts is likely to result in increased activity in any elements in which the two concepts happen to overlap. With respect to metaphor, this correlation of activity will increase the likelihood that analogous aspects of the paired elements will be noticed. The power of parallelism in literature is due to the way mutual activation creates the neural conditions prerequisite for commonalities to create activation strong enough to break through to the surface of attention.

When writing, the writer is simply editing the products of her own mind (cf. Edelman & Tononi 2000: 182). She selects the most useful trinkets from among the flotsam and jetsam that bob up from the sea of her unconscious. By the time they are selected, even before they have been selected, the fusion of style and substance is already complete, because everything in the mind is connected to something else or it wouldn't be there in the first place. The essence of the conceptual is connectivity. Even in what one might call a "jabberwocky" situation, when an author apparently spontaneously creates some nonsense word "at random," the author's creative intuitions are informed by countless linguistic and cultural constraints outside of conscious awareness. Henry James was correct in this sense. Style does not involve choosing a certain "form" and then bringing appropriate "content" in later at one's convenience, but choosing an already fused element with both semantic and formal properties that either match the author's desired result as a totality or do not.

Cognitive Parallelism, Repetition, and Style

In visual art, painters and sculptors can straightforwardly create a sense of balance in the visual medium by adjusting the spatial orientation of whichever two components they hope to be viewed in parallel. When viewers of the artwork focus their visual attention first on one component and then the other, their eyes move "so that the object of interest is imaged on the fovea of each eye" which implies that "most of the time we are paying attention to something imaged on our fovea" (Bear et al. 2001: 661). Nevertheless, in many cases the relationship between the two objects may also be noticed as a pair if both objects are close enough together to be simultaneously present in the viewer's broader field of vision.

While authors can control the reader's conceptual viewpoint easily enough by mentioning one aspect and then the other in the text, readers may not notice the parallelism unless some aspect of the pairing is sufficiently foregrounded to emphasize the implied relationship. There are a number of ways this can be achieved, including the foregrounding of grammatical or other linguistic features for each item by way of repetition. With respect to a particular poem by Emily Dickinson, Freeman notes that parallelism is used to create a sense of expectancy in the reader because "[t]he parallelisms throughout the poem adhere to a fairly strict pattern of exact equivalences in chiasmic form" (Freeman 2002: 30). As readers sense such morphological or lexical repetitions, they become aware of the parallelism. Finally, when suddenly the parallelism is broken by an unexpected variation in the pattern, foregrounding of the unaligned item results.

The key point to keep in mind is that creating such a balanced counter-point effect in a literary context is impossible without some type of repetition. This repetition may be accomplished in a number of ways, including visually (by way of fonts and page layouts), auditorily (though end rhyme or alliteration), or through less prominent conceptual association (achieved by juxtaposing lexical items that are not clearly related but which have links with conceptual content that clearly is). The first two types of repetition attract reader attention through the apparatus of sense perception while the third, although using lexical items to access the parallelism, does not rely on auditory or other features of the lexical items to accomplish it. Upon reflection, the third case represents a creative manipulation of subconscious cognitive functions to instantiate noticeable semantic symmetry in the narrative. Examples of such parallelism that are not necessarily foregrounded in the apparatus of perception include conceptual metaphor and the recapitulation of conceptual themes through repetition.

The visual and auditory modes of sensory perception both play a part in "selective attention," the neural strategy used to help humans differentially process simultaneous sources of information (Bear et al. 2001: 659). As we move on to note the associational aspects which may lead to an upsurge in neural activity and thereby garner attention, we must keep in mind that these conceptual aspects are always initially cued by some kind of perceptual input. Parallelisms found in poetry often have grammatical, visual, and auditory elements that elicit attention not simply because the author desires to instantiate a parallelism on the form plane but because language is the surest way to ignite and coordinate the fireworks of conceptual activity.

Parallelisms may be presented by way of language, but such parallelisms often do not end at the linguistic level (cf. Hiraga 2005: 41-45). Lodge has asserted that "[s]uccessful poetry is that which manages to fulfill all the requirements of a complex, purely formal pattern of sound and at the same time to seem an utterly inevitable expression of its meaning" (Lodge 1977: 89). Putting Lodge's observation into neural terms, when a poetic work fails to ignite conceptual associations in proportion to the effects it achieves in the apparatus of perception, readers may become aware of this imbalance. Such a poem runs a high risk of being labeled doggerel.

So while content and form are inseparable in practice, the author still may have a desire for a certain stylistic result. Such desires are complex products of conceptualization. In long experience with language, various categories of style develop that the author will have access to during the linguistic item selection process. Style is not only determined by choices, however, but can also be strongly influenced by conventionalized neural routines. In their book on writing style, Thomas and Turner state, "[w]e are trapped by our unconscious styles if we cannot recognize them as styles. When all of our styles are effectively default styles, we choose without knowing we are choosing and so cannot recognize the practical possibility of alternative styles" (Thomas & Turner 1994: 12). Consequently, in a cognitive literary framework, the "poetic" value of a text is located not only narrowly in the author's skill in manipulating the reader's attention through "formal" and semantic properties of the text (cf. Tabakowska 1993: 24), but also broadly in the poetic aspects resulting from myriad unconscious default decisions.

Radial Categories and Style

Fish has claimed that when literary scholars attempt to detect stylistic effects that compel reader attention they "are forced to deny literary status to works whose function is in part to convey information or offer propositions about the real world" (Fish 1980: 104) and will fail in their attempt as "properties so identified turn out to be found in texts not considered literary, or when obviously literary texts do not display the specified properties" (Fish 1980: 98). The claims Fish makes will only be true if one attempts to strictly define literature according to its function or according to the presence or absence of this or that literary value. Fortunately, cognitive linguistics does not need to use the sort of strict definitions that Fish apparently believes would be required.

According to prototype theory (e.g. Lakoff 1987: 7, 39-57), psychological experiments show that the conceptual categories humans use are not "definitional." That is, category boundaries are not strictly and logically delimited to result in clear distinctions (like dictionary definitions), but rather include some examples within categories that are more representative of the category than others.

Representative members of a category are considered to be more "prototypical." For example, birds that fly (like sparrows and ducks) are generally deemed to be more prototypical of the category "bird" than birds that do not (ostriches and penguins). Since prototypical members within a certain category tend to be "at the center" of our conceptualization of that category, such categories, with good examples at the center and other less good examples on the periphery, have been called "radial categories." Because penguins and ostriches do not fly, they fall on the periphery of our conceptualization of birds, but nevertheless they are members of the category. For this reason, when people deem a work literary (or not) they probably do so not according to some literary scholar's constricting definition but according to a flexible combination of conscious and subconscious judgments.

While the conceptual categories we use everyday are flexible enough to adapt to changes in the environment, in fact they are relatively stable over groups. Gibbs mentions a study in which one group of participants were asked to produce the features for a certain category. He notes, "[p]eople's judgments of feature validity should have varied considerably if people had varying underlying knowledge of a category" (Gibbs 1994: 53). In fact, when a new group of subjects was asked whether the properties listed by the previous group were valid or not, there was nearly perfect agreement about which features were valid.

In the same way, the category that we call literature will have a center and a periphery, and it will include works that tend to have certain identifiable features. It may be a moving center and an unstable periphery. The identifiable features of literature may only be relevant to a certain particular group. In this sense, the results of cognitive linguistic research into literature will not normally be able to offer universal findings applicable to literature in all places at all times. And if any truly universal aspects of literature are found and statistically verified, they will not be universal because they are particularly literary but because they are generally cognitive.

Visual Leveraging of Attention

Normally when literary researchers mention "formal" aspects of literature, they are primarily concerned with auditory phenomena (even for literature that tends to be read silently). Strictly speaking, however, literary "form" cannot be equated with phonology.

Hiraga has extensively documented how visual aspects of form (specifically iconicity) abound in both English-language and Japanese poetry (Hiraga 2005: 91-126). She makes a compelling case for the visual iconicity in George Herbert's "Easter Wings" (Herbert 1880: 34-35) in which the graphic layout of the published poem takes the form of wings on the printed page. She further shows how the author can manipulate subtle aspects of a reader's understanding of a poem by manipulating visual aspects (layout, type size, and fonts) of the poem's presentation (Hiraga 2005: 96-97). While not addressing the issue directly, she hints that calligraphy (the medium closely associated with the development of poetry traditions in both China and Japan) may yet prove another case in which the visual aspect of literature is not a dispensable facet of expression but an integral part of the work that cannot be ignored (Hiraga 2005: 238).

Another intriguing aspect, which I do not have the space to mention except in passing, is the difference between vertically and horizontally aligned typeface. Unlike English, which nearly always reads from left to right (there are some extremely rare poetic exceptions; cf. Hiraga 2005: 58), Japanese can be read from left to right, top to bottom, and very occasionally right to left. Literature in book form is generally formatted with each line of text extending from the top of the page to the bottom with each line thereafter ordered from right to left across pages. Japanese students in my translation classes have told me that when they read Japanese language literary texts which are not formatted vertically, they feel as if some intangible literary quality is missing from the text.

Auditory Leveraging of Attention

Poetry has often been associated with phonological phenomena despite the fact that auditory aspects are not as predominant in English language poetry as they once were. Looking ahead to a forum and various workshops on the topic "The Sound of Poetry, the Poetry of Sound" at the 2006 MLA convention, Perloff noted that the idea of "lyric poetry" originated in musical tradition, with etymological roots in the Greek word *lyra*, meaning lyre (Perloff 2006: 3). Various "musical" aspects (or at least subtle auditory aspects) found in literary works seem to be a very central part of an author's style. Translator Gregory Rabassa notes:

> In Spanish, [author Gabriel] García Márquez's words so often have the ring of prose poetry. They are always the right words because their meaning is enhanced by their sound and the way in which they are strung together in rhythmic cohesion. (Rabassa 2005: 98)

THE REASON FOR RHYME   *63*

Umberto Eco has found a similar "rhythmic cohesion" in the poetry of Eugenio Montale. Apparently hoping to allow the world to experience what he has experienced in Montale's poetry, Eco opines:

> A translation must preserve the textual rhythm. But that is not enough. As I have said in the previous chapters, many substances of expression are displayed on the expression plane and many of them are not specifically linguistic (such as metre and many phonosymbolic values). Metre is so independent from the structure of a given language that the same metric scheme can migrate from one language to another. (Eco 2003: 150)

Eco goes on from here to note how some translators of Montale fail to respect the original meter. While Eco may indeed have a point in the case of Montale's translation into other European languages, I don't believe that he fully realizes the problems involved in attempting to translate the meter of an Italian poem into non-European languages such as Japanese or Chinese. Meter is not a facet of language that can be added on or elided at the poet's whim. Meter flows from the form of a language organically and so a few more minutes of planning on the part of a translator cannot hope to compensate for differences in languages that are separated by thousands of years of linguistic evolution.

Although occasionally forced to study language in an artificial and grammar-oriented fashion, humans generally do not gain the majority of their linguistic knowledge from school textbooks. In the case of native speakers of a language, the intuitive knowledge of language that they, as a community, share, is primarily absorbed through a drawn-out, daily linguistic apprenticeship. This is the case for literature, as well, at least for literature in a broad "written cultural tradition" sense.

While Americans may or may not remember whatever classroom instruction they may or may not have received on the humorous poetic form called "limerick," they recognize the meter intuitively. Many native English speakers can even quickly compose a limerick on the spur of the moment and do so with confidence that they understand the form.

> Example 4.1
>
> There once was an arrogant waiter
>
> who brought the food later and later.
>
> His tips grew so small
>
> he brought nothing at all
>
> so the restaurant decided to cater.

Using the original limerick above as an example, I once attempted to teach a class of high-level students of English at a Japanese university how to compose a limerick. The results were astonishing.

Extremely bright students with huge vocabularies, students that would in a matter of weeks successfully complete long, fully documented English research papers in their respective disciplines, were not able to tell me with confidence how many syllables were in the word "limerick." The most popular answer was four because the Japanese transliteration of the word, *rimerikku*, has either four or five syllables depending on whether one counts the glottal stop, which is phonetically represented along with the other voiced syllables in written Japanese. The students, all quick learners, went on to figure things out and a few even wrote some rather funny limericks. Strictly speaking, though, most of the meters finally produced were not even close to achieving that genuine limerick lilt.

Of course being unable to choose a meter and stick to it over the length of a poem apparently puts them in the same literary ranks as Milton. According to pioneer cognitive stylistics proponent, Reuven Tsur, "[a]n iambic pentameter line is supposed to consist of regularly alternating unstressed and stressed syllables. In the first one hundred sixty five lines of *Paradise Lost* there are only two such lines" (Tsur 2002: 310; cf. Tsur 1998: 24). Tsur proceeds to mention a naive idea prevalent among poetic researchers: when they think they are measuring "the rhythm of a poem" they are in fact only measuring a performance of it. "When the linguistic and versification patterns conflict, they are accommodated in a pattern of performance, such that both are perceptible simultaneously" (Tsur 2002: 311). It becomes apparent that one reason the Japanese limerick composers were having so much trouble composing lay not in the formal rules I gave them (that a limerick's rhyming pattern should run A-A-B-B-A with each A-line having three beats and each B-line having two beats) but in an "unwritten rule" of limerick performance that I did not even realize I knew myself, namely that if the number syllables and stresses in a limerick do not naturally correspond to the anticipated rhythm pattern, adjust one's performance so as to cram them in.

Why is it that such complex, implicit, and apparently culture-bound values are such an integral part of English language poetry? Perhaps another famous English poetry form will give us a clue. According to Schwartz, blank verse "comes close to the natural speaking rhythms of English but raises it above the ordinary without sounding artificial (unlike the "singsong" effect produced by dialogue in rhyme)"..."[and] is used mainly for passionate, lofty or momentous occasions and for introspection; it may suggest a refinement in character" (Schwartz). Judging from this particular explanation, it would seem that blank verse is written in such a way as to sound pleasing to a native English speaker's ear but to do so without being too noticeable. English as an everyday language undoubtedly has certain rhythm patterns. Poets, over time, are likely to pick up on certain felicitous patterns (such as the patterns found in blank verse) and put these to creative use. It seems evident that characteristics of the language itself tend to determine the patterns that appeal to speakers of that language.

Schwartz's characterization of rhyme as a "sing-song" effect is also illuminating. Unlike the complex syllabification system found in English, rhyme is a concept that is naturally present in the Japanese language, although it is used somewhat differently. Japanese onomatopoeic expressions are typically constructed by way of exact phonological repetition. *Bata-bata* expresses the sound of a helicopter or a flag waving in the breeze. *Kasa-kasa* can indicate the rustling of leaves or a feeling of dryness. *Pachi-pachi* indicates the sound of clapping. In short, both native English speakers and native Japanese speakers have rhyme detection apparatus among their preset cognitive capabilities which, although potentially lacking in ability to detect rhyme in a foreign language, at least can detect rhyme in the first language once it has been learned.

The most interesting thing about end rhyme in the English literary tradition is not that it exists. From a statistical point of view, even random strings of words would eventually produce some noticeable end rhyme. The most interesting thing about end rhyme is that a certain subset of humanity appreciates this effect to the extent that it does, and that the borders that distinguish this subset of humanity from other subsets are not primarily cultural boundaries but linguistic ones. From nursery rhymes to gangster rap, end rhyme has become so thoroughly associated with the popular perception of "poetry" in cultures that use English that many postmodern poets feel obliged to rebel against its constraints as a matter of principle.

This strong urge to rhyme words at the end of lines in poetry, however, is far from universal. This is not to say that people of some other cultural and linguistic traditions cannot detect such rhyming. As with the case of Japanese onomatopoeic language, in their own language at least, they can. They simply fail to attach a similar level of importance to it. What causes this profound difference between native speakers of English and native speakers of Japanese?

Spoken Japanese has a relatively limited syllabic repertoire (cf. Hiraga 2005: 168-169). There are only five vowels sounds in Japanese, *a, i, u, e,* and *o,* and these are combined with a relatively limited set of available consonants to form the primary syllabary used in modern Japanese, *hiragana*. In the Japanese "alphabet," the first five characters, *a, i, u, e,* and *o,* are followed by *ka, ki, ku, ke,* and *ko,* with almost all of the remaining characters being pronounced according to the same consonant-vowel combination pattern. As a result, the permutations of vowel-consonant combinations are limited and, relative to English, somewhat monotonous. The fact that the number of sounds in the Japanese-language pronunciation repertoire is relatively limited causes them to be repeated frequently, even in ordinary, everyday language.

These language differences alone can account for the great disparity in attention with respect to end rhyme for native Japanese speakers and native speakers of English. The very frequency of such naturally occurring "rhyme" in Japanese produces a relatively high proportion of internal and end rhyme. As has been noted in the previous chapter, when a certain kind of stimuli is constantly available, the neural system becomes desensitized to that type of stimuli. Conversely, because the English language has more vowels and consonants and freely places consonants both before and after vowel sounds, there are many more permutations of vowel-consonant combinations and so there is less likelihood that English will naturally produce rhyme in everyday language. This dearth of naturally occurring rhyme in English assures that native speakers will be sensitized to it and therefore will have a low threshold for noticing the effect.

In the Japanese "poetic" tradition, there are instances where end and internal rhyme are used but these poetic aspects are not as central to the concept of "poetry" in Japanese. The differences do not end there. In fact, two key concepts that have historically been at the center of the radial category of Western poetry (meter and the strong, beat-oriented rhythmic orientation of verse) are, if not completely irrelevant to Japanese poetry, entirely peripheral. On the other hand, some other poetic categories appreciated by native English speakers may be more viable when translated. It would be useful to compare English and Japanese conceptualizations of literature to ascertain which literary values are interculturally viable and which literary values are not.

Pilot Study

To more clearly determine the relative viability of aesthetic effects associated with English language literature, I first did a pilot study with the assistance of 18 Japanese university students in my Japanese-English translation course. The participants were shown 23 terms related to the aesthetic analysis of English literature and asked to evaluate whether the same effect would be possible to achieve in a Japanese translation. Terms were rated using a 3-point Likert scale ("impossible to translate," "not sure," "possible to translate"). Some problems occurred during the survey because many subjects could not understand certain terms even with definitions provided.

One example of a problematic term was "accentual meter." To understand accentual meter one must have an understanding of strong speech stresses. Japanese stresses tend to be much less prominent than those in English and furthermore, Japanese poetic forms such as *haiku* or *tanka* are not arranged rhythmically but according to precise *mora* counts. Because English language and Japanese poetic forms are fundamentally different in this respect, students did not feel they understood the idea of "accentual meter" well enough to respond to the question.

In designing a follow-up survey, various problems occurring in the pilot study were taken into consideration. First, it was deemed necessary to eliminate categories that had been problematic in the pilot study (e.g. the previously mentioned "accentual meter" and relatively difficult to explain terms such as "metafiction"). Secondly, the 3-point Likert scale used in the pilot study did not allow subtle differences in ratings to be evaluated, so it was decided that a richer rating scale should be used. Thirdly, since all of the subjects in the pilot study had participated in my course on English-Japanese translation, there was a possibility that participant responses had been influenced by my teaching. On the other hand, there was a concern that participants without experience in translation would be unable to rate the terms in an informed manner. To compensate for this, I decided to administer the survey to the students of three different classes, two of which were unrelated to translation or language study.

English Literature Values Intercultural Viability Survey

Method

The survey was administered to 22 university students. Students received class credit for participation. The results of 3 incomplete surveys were discarded. Participants were asked to rate their own level of translation experience, response options including "experienced," "somewhat experienced," little experience," and "no experience." The participants were shown 12 English literary terms (supplemented by a Japanese language definition of the English term) and asked to evaluate whether the literary effect indicated by the term would be possible to achieve in a Japanese translation. Terms were rated using a 7-point Likert scale. Response options ranged from 1 (completely impossible) to 7 (completely possible) with an "unsure" option at the midpoint of the scale.

Results

Responses were analyzed independently for each literary term and significant results were further analyzed to determine which Likert scale rating level(s) led to the significant result. Literary terms for which the rating "completely possible" had a significant number of responses were "climax," (x^2 (6, N= 19)=13.05, p<.05) and "irony," (x^2 (6, N=19)=20.42, p<.01). Literary terms for which the rating "possible" had a significant number of responses were "characterization," (x^2 (6)= 32.94, p<.01), "local color," (x^2 (6, N=19)= 15.263, p<.05) which also had a significant number of responses for "somewhat possible," and "metaphor," (x^2 (6, N=19)= 15.26, p<.05) which had a significant number of responses for "somewhat possible," as well. Literary terms for which the rating "somewhat possible" had a significant number of responses were "parallelism" (x^2 (6, N=19)=21.89, p<.01) which had a significant number of responses for "unsure" as well, and "end rhyme" (x^2 (6, N=19)= 26.33, p<.01) which also had a significant low number of responses for "possible." The only literary term that had a significant number of responses for the rating "somewhat impossible" was "rhythm" (x^2 (6, N=19)=17.474, p<.01). Results for "alliteration," "atmosphere," "assonance," and "onomatopoeia" were non-significant.

Means and standard deviations for each literary term (in descending order from highest to lowest mean for all participants) are found in Table 4.1. For each literary term, a chi-square test was used to compare the responses of subjects with and without translation experience but there were no significant differences.

Table 4.1   English Literature Values Intercultural Viability Survey Results

Term	All Participants		Trans. Experience		NoTrans.Experience	
	Mean	SD	Mean	SD	Mean	SD
characterization	5.95	0.87	6.00	0.74	5.86	0.69
irony	5.68	1.42	5.75	1.42	5.57	1.27
metaphor	5.53	1.54	5.58	1.24	5.43	0.98
climax	5.37	1.56	5.58	1.62	5.00	1.15
atmosphere	5.37	1.51	5.42	1.44	5.29	1.25
parallelism	5.00	1.92	5.25	0.97	4.57	0.79
local color	4.74	1.67	4.50	1.38	5.14	0.69
onomatopoeia	4.47	2.47	4.08	1.83	5.14	1.21
end rhyme	4.37	1.16	4.42	1.16	4.29	1.89
rhythm	4.21	2.88	3.75	1.66	5.00	1.15
alliteration	4.11	2.06	3.75	1.96	4.71	1.11
assonance	3.68	1.80	3.17	1.80	4.57	1.72

Discussion

It was expected that there would be significant differences between responses of participants with translation experience and those without but, rather surprisingly, no significant differences were evident. Judging from the results in Table 4.1, the difference between the two groups was one of confidence in making judgments rather than altogether differing views of translation. The mean response values for participants with translation experience ranged from 6.00 to 3.17 (range=2.83) while the range for those without translation experience was a narrower 5.86 to 4.57 (range =1.29).

Looking more closely, means in the range from 6.0 to 5.25 for participants with translation experience invariably corresponded to lower means for those without translation experience while means from 4.5 to 3.17 for participants with translation experience corresponded to higher means for those without experience, with one exception. For the term "end rhyme" alone the mean of the experienced translators' responses was higher than that of their inexperienced counterparts. Standard deviations also point toward the interpretation of data just mentioned, the standard deviations for experienced translators being greater than for those without experience, again with the exception of "end rhyme." From these results, it may be hypothesized that participants with experience tended to be more confident about their opinions concerning translation and therefore more emphatic in their judgments, whether in the direction of "possible" or "impossible."

Upon reflection it stands to reason that the responses of students who self-report little or no experience with translation would differ only minimally from those with experience. Most Japanese university students, during the course of their compulsory education before university entrance, have at one time or another learned English by way of the so-called "grammar-translation" method. For this reason, the typical Japanese university student has a relatively extensive understanding of English to Japanese translation issues. Even in the absence of any training specifically tailored to translation, Japanese university students tend already to possess the English skills necessary to make informed judgments concerning English to Japanese translation.

With respect to general trends, "climax," "irony," "characterization," "local color," and "metaphor" are terms that participants judged to be relatively more viable with respect to Japanese translation, although the mean for "local color" is somewhat lower than the other four. "Parallelism" also tended to be viewed as viable in Japanese translation, if to a lesser extent. While "rhythm" yielded the only significant negative result among the remaining terms, this outcome was likely due to the nature of the survey administered. The 7-point Likert scale tended to spread both positive and negative judgments concerning a term's viability over one of the three positive or three negative options, thereby making it relatively unlikely that a statistically significant number of responses would occur for any given option. In fact, "onomatopoeia," "end rhyme," "alliteration," "rhythm," and "assonance" all displayed means at the lower end of the various ranges, indicating that these terms tended to be seen as less viable than the others. Changing the scale to a 4- or 5-point scale would likely lead to significant (probably negative) results for these terms, as well.

The results of analysis for "end rhyme" are intriguing because the term had a significant high number of responses for "somewhat possible" and a significant low number of responses for "possible" simultaneously. Furthermore, despite the significant "somewhat possible" judgment, the mean was in the low end of the range. One explanation for these unusual results would be to hypothesize that the participants all judged "end rhyme" to be technically possible to achieve but nevertheless hesitated to rate it highly because the resulting effect in the Japanese translation would not approach the intensity of the effect in the original English work. In fact, this hypothesis fits perfectly with the observation made previously in this chapter regarding how the limited number of Japanese vowel-consonant permutations creates naturally occurring rhyme that leads to desensitization through everyday language use. This situation makes end rhyme not only possible but statistically prevalent even in the absence of poetic artifice and thereby raises the critical threshold necessary for rhyme to function as an attention-getting auditory device in Japanese.

It was somewhat surprising to notice that "parallelism," an aspect of cognition that seems to play a fundamental role in both perception and conceptual association, did not receive a higher rating for intercultural viability. It is possible that students had a clear recognition of the fact that English language poetry tends to use more overt types of parallelism than *haiku* or other traditional Japanese poetic forms. In fact, *haiku* is not without aspects of parallelism, the most obvious aspect being the way that the 5-7-5 *mora* scheme aligns the 5-*mora* sections at either side of the 7-*mora* middle section. Nevertheless, the question answered on the survey did not assess whether parallelism occurs in Japanese literature or not, only whether the type of parallelism found in English literature could be *reproduced* in a Japanese literary context. Apparently, the participants felt that such a transposition would be difficult to achieve.

As a conclusion to this discussion, it should be clearly stated what this survey has shown. On the positive side, the survey has statistically demonstrated the English literature values that Japanese speakers feel are difficult to translate into Japanese. These results are only relevant for English to Japanese translation and reflect not absolute levels of difficulty but subjective *impressions* of difficulty. It is entirely possible that some aspects of literary texts have levels of complexity and types of artifice that, because they are not generally perceived, have not been factored into these *perceptions* of difficulty. Only the literary values that the participants have actually noticed will have affected their assessments.

Distinguishing Presets from Cultural Factors

Cross-referencing the results of the survey with my observations at the beginning of this chapter, there are two points that I hope will be acknowledged. First, while disparate languages have the potential to differ with one another in various ways, not all of those differences are equally insurmountable with respect to translation. Some differences will prove to be more difficult to overcome than others. Second, aspects of one language (such as alliteration or assonance) that on first inspection appear to be "surface aspects" tied to idiosyncrasies of the particular poetic tradition and therefore untranslatable, may actually be possible in the target language due to the fact that the presets of perception are recurrent. Nevertheless, due to linguistic differences, these potentially translatable "surface aspects" may be less poetically viable.

The reason that auditory phenomena such as alliteration, assonance, and end rhyme have historically been seen as central to the western conception of poetry undoubtedly lies not in poetic preferences selected at random in a given culture, nor in fundamental differences in the perceptual systems of the hearers. The differences are a logical and completely predictable natural outgrowth of the language that has produced them. Alliteration, assonance, and end rhyme are all possible in Japanese. Due to differences in the languages, however, even should they be selected as literary values, they will be used differently and are not likely to produce the same type of effects or achieve the same level of effect that they produce in English.

Associational Leveraging of Long-term Memory Resources

Prose does not fire up the reader's presets of perception the way that poetry does for a very important reason: prose tends to operate at a length of discourse that would be unsustainable for a "poetic" work. Poetry relies on noticing to stimulate perceptual activity and focus the reader's attention on the text in the short-term, but resource-depletion in the affected equipment of perception means that the level of intensity used by poetry to gain a reader's attention is impossible to sustain over an extended discourse.

As we have already seen in the previous chapter, understanding of narrative and extended discourse is a marker of intellectual maturity in humans and deficits in the capacity would not seem to enhance adaptivity. While some poetry does have great depth and may indeed accomplish some upgrade in a reader's narrative comprehension abilities, extended narrative offers decided advantages as the brain attempts to expand and develop the domains in the conceptual system. This being the case, it would only be natural that prose would tend, over time, to adapt itself less to the parameters that enable noticing and short-term memory than to the parameters of long-term associational entrenchment so as to more effectively build out the system.

In that short-term memories last "on the order of seconds to hours" (Bear et al. 2001: 741), it can be plausibly asserted that most poetry achieves its noticeable effects within the effective range of short-term memory. This is not to say that poetry has no hope of becoming integrated into long-term memory. To the extent that poetry elicits strong responses of one kind or another in the reader, aspects of the poem may become quickly seared into the reader's recall (Bear et al. 2001: 805). Nevertheless, short-term memories are called short-term memories for a reason: lacking sufficient activation they will fade and leave little synaptic evidence that they ever existed.

Among declarative memories (memories concerning facts or events), there are certain preconditions for consolidation into long-term memory. One of these is recurrent input (Edelman 1992: 104). It should not be surprising that humans are sensitive to repetition. After all, as Feldman notes, "[m]ost life processes, like the amoeba recognizing its food, happen repeatedly. They are iterative processes, with a sequence of states, returning to the initial state to begin the process again" (Feldman 2006: 46).

The biological basis for long-term memory is different from that of short-term memory because making memory permanent requires the construction of new protein molecules in the synaptic membranes of the neurons involved (Feldman 2006: 79). Creation of these molecules is not instantaneous but rather requires hours for completion. For this reason, repetition after time elapsed is one key to long-term memory (Edelman & Tononi 2000: 95). The process by which enhancements in the strength of stimulated synapses transform short-term memories into long-term memories is called "long-term potentiation" (Bear et al. 2001: 791; cf. Feldman 2005: 80).

Repetition of all kinds, as used by authors in literature then, seems to have a dual function. On the one hand it cues attention and on the other hand, as attention is cued, neural activity in the related areas spike, thereby increasing the likelihood of consolidation into long-term memory.

On the Cognitive Rewards that Accompany Repetition

Talking of consolidation into long-term memory is fine on the level of neurobiology, but what's in it for the reader? In poetry, readers seem to experience pleasure when they encounter ingenious combinations of perceptual effects. Is there any such "reward" for prose reading? Going back to the false dichotomy between the epicurean and the pragmatic mentioned at the beginning of the chapter, it is difficult to say that, in the end, poetry is any more epicurean than prose. In terms of pleasure, both poetry and prose are capable of causing the reader to feel pleasure but there is no guarantee that pleasure (neurally accomplished through stimulation of certain areas of the brain, the release of dopamine or serotonin, etc.; cf. Bear et al. 2001: 598-604) is the only motivating factor for reading. Suffice to say that the human body has built-in incentive systems that reward both perceptional activation and conceptual development, the previously mentioned habituation and sensitization effects being among these. While reading literature may be a relatively pleasant experience, in neural terms it is nearly impossible to distinguish between epicurean and pragmatic motivations for reading literature.

After reviewing formal aspects of visual and auditory stimuli and corresponding organization as an outcome in the associational system, is there any conclusion to be found? After my skeptical appraisal of nifty dichotomies, I will not offer another. What I will offer is an interrelated pair of (non-mutually exclusive) constraints: attention and consolidation. Prose authors, while maintaining the right to utilize every trick and gimmick that poets have ever conceived of to attract the reader's attention, generally tend not to use these attention-getting effects in a sustained way due to neural limitations in the reader's apparatus of perception. To compensate, they tend to provide conceptual content that is gradually consolidated through semantic artifice, including macro-level conceptual parallelisms (such as diffused-domain extended metaphors) and recapitulation of themes.

Poetry and other differing poetic forms such as *haiku*, whether by way of highly "imagable" auditory or visual stimuli, seem designed to attract the reader's attention quickly and monopolize it, albeit for a short period of time. There is an intriguing pejorative word used to describe verbal stimulus arrays that haplessly mimic longer literary forms by failing to provide attention-grabbing stimuli at a sufficiently brisk pace: prosaic. Consequently, if a poetic work should be pronounced prosaic, it is the worst possible criticism.

Concerning Cycles of Style

So if these aspects of attention contribute to our appreciation of an artistic work, shouldn't that mean that creativity will inevitably be a one-way street in the direction of excess and flamboyant expression? If artistic merit were judged according to skill in manipulating a single facet of attention alone, this might be the case, but the presets of perception and other cognitive features work in coordination and compete with each other for limited neural resources.

The neural presets determine whether a reader has the potential to perceive assonance in a poem but the reader's culture and personal experiences will determine whether that assonance will be noticed and, if noticed, deemed to be literary. While cultures cannot control the presets of perception, they do influence matters of individual taste.

Such is the case with the present tendency for many "serious" American poets to ignore the auditory presets of attention. With respect to this trend, poet and critic Dana Gioia has remarked:

> Influenced by print culture's habit of silent reading and its typographical bias toward a text's visual identity on the page, contemporary literary poets often neglect or underplay the auditory elements of their verse. Too overt or apprehensible a verbal pattern seems old-fashioned to many poets. (Gioia 2004: 17)

Gioia goes on to point out rap music's tendency to identify strong, interesting rhyme with the flamboyant personal identity of the rapper. The difference between written literature and recorded rap are partially explained by the differences in their formats. On the other hand, though, insofar as yesterday's pop culture often becomes the "high" culture of tomorrow (Pinker 2002: 403), perhaps there is a literary wave developing. Perhaps the current generation of poets, with their tendency to problematize the mundane and their unwillingness to bow to convention, stylistic or otherwise, are setting the table for a backlash of stylized, orthodox, sentimental poetry.

Art historian John Walford has observed:

> As we look at art across time, we can expect to find both continuity of human interest and changes in artistic style. Radical changes generally signal a significant shift in the interests and outlooks of both artists and their audience. (Walford 2002: 13)

This statement is a mainstream viewpoint that properly interprets cultural concerns and shifts in the social environment as key motivating factors for aesthetic change; but it does not account for the unmoving boundaries laid down by the embodied presets of aesthetic appreciation. Artistic "presets" in the realm of linguistic communication function, first, by resulting in particular instances of communication for individuals, and then cumulatively, as records of such successful language use. Literature, then, is a record of the constantly adapting strategies used to capture the human imagination by the lexical leveraging of attention.

But isn't it possible to write poetry ignoring the limits of attention, or to write prose in short form that does not use long-term memory inducing strategies? Wouldn't it be possible to ignore the constraints of human cognition? Certainly, but not all of them at once.

The exceptions we find are either outliers, like James Joyce's *Ulysses* (Joyce 1922), or, in the case of Arthur Rimbaud's prose poems (e.g. Rimbaud 1886), not really exceptions, at all. *Ulysses* is a highly allusive long-form poem, extended beyond the bounds of normal human perception; for this reason it is not read by normal humans. From the very beginning, Joyce's masterpiece was a literary phenomenon generated by a narrow cross-section of sophisticated readers, an avant-garde elite displaying what one might call skills of "conspicuous concentration." On the other hand, Rimbaud's prose poems are anything but prosaic, including strong imagability, conceptual complexity, and some less prominent auditory elements (Perloff 2006: 3). Nevertheless, Rimbaud's most representative works do not include end rhyme or visually prominent versification on the page. Because he chose to limit his auditory artifice and decided not to foreground what he did include, Rimbaud's sonic effects were present but unaccounted for.

Both Joyce and Rimbaud were talented "poets" whose poetry lends credence to two key observations concerning the limits of literary creativity. Authors are only able to successfully ignore cognitive values if they emphasize other values so as to overcome the deficit created. Furthermore, although authors may succeed in capturing reader attention with a certain strategy, they will not keep it for long. As repetition leads first to attention but finally to desensitization, the human imagination is forever destined to stray onto new paths, new paths that nevertheless are walled in by the same set of cognitive constraints as the old ones.

5

WHEN WORLDS COLLIDE

Many people, people who have never done any translation at all, especially people who do not read foreign books, seem to believe that no act is so devious as winning a literary reputation by translating, that only minimal effort is required to take someone else's ideas, someone else's writings, and mechanically remove them from their left-to-right horizontal alignment [in a foreign language] and rewrite them vertically [into Japanese], that the process is not so different from the transmission of words by way of the telephone or the copying done by a scribe. Such beliefs about translation abound.

Kōtoku Shūsui

(1994: 56; Strack translation)

In chapters 2 and 3, I stressed some of the cognitive factors that make translation "possible," in however narrow a sense. In framing this book in such a way I did not mean to imply that, in all or even most cases, such general cognitive processes will determine every outcome. Scarpa correctly notes:

The fact that linguistic categorization is motivated by general, and therefore universal, cognitive processes [...] does not mean that linguistic categories are universal. [...] Identical cognitive and perceptual capacities can in fact provide valid motivations for developing different conceptual systems and, whilst being motivated intralinguistically, categories are indissolubly linked to experiential factors which are culturally, historically and linguistically

82

specific. (Scarpa 2002: 141)

Because cultures and languages differ, sometimes to a greater and sometimes to a lesser extent, literary translation becomes an extremely (some would say prohibitively) complex operation. This chapter will offer a few examples of how translation, even when theoretically possible, is complicated by incompatibilities between languages and cultures.

On the Difficulty of Nouns

When one begins to look for problems that arise in translation, it is not even necessary to go to the phrase level: even the most basic types of words will suffice, nouns being the particular example I will mention here. Sometimes there may be multiple options available that the translator must choose from. For example, there are four different transliterations for the word "aerosol" in Japanese: *earozoru, eazōru, eazoru,* and *ērozoru* (Shirakawa). These four transliterations are used in various fields, including meteorology, engineering, pharmaceuticals, and manufacturing. Translators working on practical translations in different fields each established a particular transliteration which went on to become the standard transliteration for the respective industry. Which one is correct? They all are, depending on which cross-section of Japanese speakers one is translating for.

Inexperienced translators often assume transliterating the names of people and places into the phonetic system of the target language to be one of the easiest aspects of translation. Noted Japanese translator, Sadanori Bekku, has been outspoken on this issue:

> Students often ask me, "What do you struggle with while you're translating?" and if I reply, "Well, now that I think about it, maybe proper nouns," they say "No way!" or "You've got to be kidding" and fail to see my point. These

men and women seem to be under the impression that when a lot of proper nouns turn up, troublesome aspects of translation decrease, allowing them to relax. Such is the shallow thinking of amateurs. (Bekku 1994: 237; Strack Translation)

What kind of problems is Bekku referring to? Let's consider a few.

It's easy to say "when in Rome do as the Romans" but what if the Romans travel to New York by way of Tokyo? When translating a Japanese text that refers to Italy into English, should a reference to the Japanese *Rōma* be translated to the commonly used Anglicization "Rome" or the relatively well-known transliteration "Roma"? And if the translator does happen to choose Roma, does this choice necessitate a similar decision for Firenze, which English speakers tend to recognize by the Anglicization "Florence"? Naples or Napoli? Milan or Milano? Is it permissible to mix styles on a case by case basis? (c.f. Bekku 1994: 237-239)

And what about historical places that no longer use the same name? What about Petrograd? In English, it was previously St. Petersburg, and then Petrograd, and then Leningrad, and now is St. Petersburg once again. Logically, it seems that, outside of Soviet era literature, it should be called St. Petersburg. And yet in a few different translations of Anna Karenina (Tolstoy 1961; Tolstoy 1983; Tolstoy 2000), I notice that it is simply called "Petersburg." Is this simply an abbreviation (that many non-Russian speakers including myself) have never heard of?

What about "Port Arthur" the former Russian concession in China, renamed "*Ryojun*" during the Japanese colonial period, and now relatively unknown as *Lushun*? Japanese readers are as unlikely to know Port Arthur as English speakers are to know *Ryojun* and neither group will know Lushun. Furthermore, while the name Port Arthur certainly has a nice English-sounding ring to it (for obvious reasons), in this respect it succeeds so well that it doesn't

84

sound like a place in China at all.

Sometimes translators walk unknowingly into linguistic traps that only a few native speakers of the source language would be able to avoid. When translating from Japanese into English, one commonly encounters uncommon readings of Chinese logographs. For example, the *kanji* combination 青木 ("blue tree"; a common surname) is typically pronounced *Aoki*, but in Kōbe there is a place-name with the same *kanji* that is pronounced *Ōgi* (Nakano 1994: 174). If the translator happens to be from the Kansai region of Japan, she will be in luck and the English transliteration will be transcribed accurately. Only unflagging diligence on the part of the Japanese to English translator in checking the pronunciations of Japanese names and place names, even when they seem to be obvious, will eliminate such mistakes. More ambiguous is the question of what to do about the names of lakes, rivers and islands. When the *kanji* for lake (pronounced *ko* in many cases) is included in a combination like 琵琶湖, should it be translated as Lake Biwa, Biwako, or the seemingly redundant Lake Biwako? Despite much debate, Japan's translators have yet to reach a consensus on this issue.

The problems faced when translating personal names can cause much greater problems. What does a translator do if names in a work of fiction seem to have been chosen to subtly express some overall meaning conveyed by the narrative generally? In his examination of the origins of modern Japanese literature, *Dawn to the West*, Donald Keene remarks about Futabatei Shimei's influential work *Ukigumo* (1887; *The Drifting Cloud*):

As in so many Meiji novels, the names of the characters were apparently intended to suggest their roles. Bunzō is the man of *bun*, the Confucian-minded literatus; Noboru's name means "to climb"; and one meaning of the character used for Osei's name is "impulse". (Keene 1984: 110)

WHEN WORLDS COLLIDE   *85*

Keene mentions this phenomenon only with respect to Meiji era Japanese literature, but such artifice is common in many world literatures. To give one example, Hemingway's main protagonist in *For Whom the Bell Tolls* (1940) is named
Robert Jordan, "Jordan" being the name of a Biblical river (2 Sam. 17: 22; Matt.
3:6). His name prefigures the fact that he will figuratively "cross the river Jordan"
by dying at the story's close (cf. Strack 2000: 113-114).

Translating such semantically loaded names almost inevitably leads
either to loss of subtle clues that facilitate interpretation or loss of the name's pronunciation which is organically linked to the broad cultural background inhab-
ited by the character. As the local culture cannot be easily separated from the
character's identity, it would take a tremendous amount of daring to eschew
transliteration and translate the Japanese name *Bunzō* in *Ukigumo* as "Literary-
man" (or perhaps "Letterman"?). Similarly, when translating the surname
Jordan into Japanese, the translator must choose between the normal American
pronunciation of Jordan and the transliteration of the river name used in Japanese
translations of the Bible, "*Yorudan*" (*Kyūyaku seisho* 459; *Shinyaku seisho* 3).
Not surprisingly, in both cases, actual translators of these works, Ryan for
Ukigumo (Futabatei 1967) and Ōkubo for *For Whom the Bell Tolls* (Hemingway
1994), chose the less resonant but safer alternative.

Cultural Situations and Social Contexts

According to Japanese language educator Shigekatsu Yamauchi, "[w]hile
English is very particular about number (singular and plural) and gender (he or
she), Japanese is not. This enables Japanese to avoid worrying about the kinds
of linguistic gymnastics often seen in contemporary number- and gender-neu-
tral English statements" (Yamauchi). Of course, from another perspective, this
particular instance represents an exception to the rule. It is nearly impossible to
use the Japanese language without implicitly acknowledging one's own gender
and position in the social hierarchy with respect to the addressee. Feldman, notes

that some languages "explicitly encode the social relation between the speaker and the hearer" to such an extent that "the social system, the conceptual system, and the rules of grammar reinforce one another so strongly that it makes no sense to try to say which is influencing the other" (Feldman 2006: 193). This is likely the case with Japanese. While English has its share of assumptions implicit to language as well, in general, it tends to be less hierarchical than Japanese, allowing speakers somewhat "neutral ground" on which to converse on relatively equal terms. This difference between the two languages and cultures can cause difficulties for translators.

In Ariyoshi Sawako's psychologically complex story *Ki no kawa* (Ariyoshi 1959) tensions between characters surface less in explicit messages conveyed than in the extent to which characters abide by or ignore the implicit gender-specific, hierarchical rules that govern conversation in Japanese. *Ki no kawa* includes the story of Hana, a new bride who is trying to adapt to living with her in-laws, the Matani family. In one scene, Hana's maid, Toku, offers to fetch tea for Kōsaku, Hana's new brother-in-law, but she does so in a rather confrontational way that does not recognize his position (Ariyoshi 1959: 68-69). For this lapse in stylistic propriety she is (only figuratively) "fired" by Hana and sent back to work again for Hana's grandmother Toyono at her previous place of service.

In a real sense, the maid's inappropriate language functions simultaneously as a window on her soul and as a window on the greater social tension in the story: the faithful maid was using a forceful communication strategy to increase the standing of the young wife (and her extended family) with her new in-laws. Hana did not appreciate this ostentatious show of loyalty.

To mistranslate such a passage is to risk turning Toku's revolt into a purely personal uprising and miss characterizing the overall social situation. Although the story may be read from a number of critical viewpoints, to the extent that the book has been written by a woman and is primarily about women,

WHEN WORLDS COLLIDE *87*

to fail to include social hierarchy- and gender-related linguistic nuances evident
in the dialogue is to eviscerate the social fabric that makes the story coherent but
also meaningful.

The world of geisha offers a slightly different but equally idiosyncratic
view of gender relations. Mishima Yukio's "*Hashizukushi*" (Mishima 1956)
includes the following passage:

Example 5.1

かな子は二十二歳で踊りの筋もいいのに、旦那運がなくて、<ruby>春秋<rt>はるあき</rt></ruby>の
恒例の踊りにもいい役がつかない。(Mishima 1956: 309)

Kanako wa nijūnisai de odori no suji mo ii no ni, danna un ga nakute,

haruaki no kōrei no odori ni mo ii yaku ga tsukanai.

Translation 5.1

Kanako, the other geisha, though only twenty-two and quite a good dancer,
had no patron and seemed fated never to be assigned a decent part in the
annual spring and autumn geisha dances. (Mishima 1966: 76; Keene
Translation)

In this passage, it is mentioned that Kanako has had no *danna un* and that she
has been unable to get one of the lead dancing parts in the seasonal dances. As
un means "luck" and *danna* generally refers to a husband, inexperienced translators (including myself a few years ago and more recently the Japanese students
in my translation classes) tend to interpret the sentence as meaning that Kanako
is unlucky in two ways: she can't find a husband and, furthermore, has not been
given a lead part in the seasonal performances. Translators who have read other
stories about geisha, however, will realize that in the *karyūkai* (花柳界; typically
translated "the pleasure quarters"), a geisha's *danna* is the patron who supports
her monetarily and is therefore entitled to varying levels of special treatment. The

patron may very well be married (to someone else) and thereby be a *danna* in both senses of the word, but in the geisha context, a *danna* usually is not the geisha's legal spouse.

With this unstated background knowledge, the translation of the narrator's statement about Kanako must be reinterpreted. The fact that she has not yet found a patron is the very reason that she has not been able to secure a good dancing part. If she succeeds in finding a (preferably rich) patron, he would presumably give her some backstage assistance so that she can obtain a better part.

In Mishima's story, the mention of the word *danna* comes and goes but in Nagai Kafū's short story *Botan no kyaku* (Nagai 1909; previously mentioned in chapter 3), the word proves to be a key to overall interpretation. In a few separate passages, the boatman who takes the travelers up the river to view the peonies refers to the narrator as *danna*. Here however, the word is used ironically. Whether the boatman innocently believes that the couple is actually married or is using the word knowingly to impudently tease the narrator is unclear. What is clear is that Kafū's ambiguous use of the word forces the reader to consider not only the nature of the couple's relationship but the nature of marriage itself. In that English virtually precludes the idea of a boatman addressing a customer in a way that highlights his social role as a "husband," the English translator must find some other way to communicate the same sense of irony. Undoubtedly some sort of compensatory measure would be possible, but will only be implemented if the translator has already realized that the two are not in fact married.

In Japanese, when people meet for the first time they are generally expected to say, "*Dōzo yorishiku onegaishimasu*," which, in word-for-word metaphrase translates to "please / [treat me] well / [I] request." While native speakers of English may in fact hope that a newly met person will treat them well, to actually say such a thing outright would border on preposterous. The statement implies a mutual acknowledgment of the speaker's utter vulnerability, a situation that the Japanese expression seems to take for granted. In English, "please be good to me" is a request that only seems appropriate as an anxious plea from one newlywed to another on their wedding night. Unless the translator hopes to foreground the great difference between communication strategies in English and Japanese (and of course this is one option available), an analogous but more functionally equivalent expression must be found.

When spoken by an "upper crust" woman of a few generations past, a functionally equivalent expression that recognizes the situational context of a first meeting might be "How do you do?" Unfortunately, this phrase would be idiosyncratic in the current American cultural setting, so much so, in fact, that the heightened sense of propriety might be taken for a joke. 21st century Americans often simply say "hello" in such situations but for the translator to select this very loose paraphrase amounts to an unconditional surrender to the cultural mores of the target language. Even the slightly more formal "nice to meet you," while perhaps not the worst choice, succeeds in stripping away most of the distinctively Japanese decorum from the original expression. Consistently we find that, while 19th century England offers the social stratification and culturally acceptable forms of reserved propriety favorable for translation of such niceties, generally speaking, Japanese culture and American culture do not match in this respect.

Scarpa asserts that "two systems are said to be incommensurable when they are so radically different that they cannot be ‘calibrated’, i.e. compared, by means of common criteria and standards" (Scarpa 2002: 135). While social stratification, attitudes toward politeness, and levels of directness appear to be extremely different in English and Japanese, the differences are differences in degree and do not preclude comparison. That is, each aspect can be understood according to mutually identifiable criteria and standards. The amount of significance attached to the various values differ from culture to culture but, insofar as a mutual category exists, there is at least hope of discovering some medium of transformation.

Koller (1992: 176) points out that, even though certain aspects of the cultural situation (e.g. political, socio-economic, historical, and geographic particulars) in the target culture may be different from those in the source culture, there are certain compensatory techniques (cf. Schäffner 2004: 1256) that the translator can use to get around the problem. One technique is transliteration (phonetically representing the problematic source language word or words in the target language) and then appending a footnote or some other kind of explanatory note, if necessary. Unfortunately, this strategy is intrusive and may distract from the text itself. Another way to deal with such differences would be to substitute a similar word or idea if one can be found. In some cases it may be possible to subtly incorporate a concise working definition of the problematic word into the text itself. When all else fails, elision of the problematic item may be possible if it seems not to be central to the text being translated.

Whenever problematic words or ideas appear, the translator should be conscious of the compensatory techniques available. The elision of content is a particularly risky strategy in literature because literary authors tend to be very "economical" with words and so it is difficult to be certain that any word or idea that seems unnecessary in the text really is. For this reason, until each of the other types of creative circumvention have been attempted and found wanting, the translator should not throw up her hands in defeat and elide content. Unconditional surrender does not leave room for negotiation, and translation, as Eco (2003) has so eloquently observed, is all about negotiation.

Cultural Differences in Conceptualization

According to translator Gregory Rabassa, the protagonist in Kafka's *The Metamorphosis* (Kafka 1915) was called in German an *ungeheuern Ungeziefer* (a monstrous vermin) that probably referred to a kind of beetle but which New Yorkers would not hesitate to call a cockroach (Rabassa 2005: 7). Takahashi

Yoshitaka, the story's Japanese translator, however, suggests that the insect in question may be a gigantic centipede (*kyodai na mukade*) (Takahashi 1952: 112). While it may be commonplace to suggest that the conceptualizations of such insects would vary with culture, in some cases the differences can be startling.

In Japan, for example, beetles are extremely popular with children (and many adults) who keep them as pets, collect them, and sell them for profit. Children watch TV shows about beetle-shaped superheroes and play video games in which the insects are made to duel in surprisingly ferocious yet somehow non-injurious beetle-on-beetle battles. For this reason, any Japanese translation to be read by present-day readers that happens to depict Kafka's insect as a beetle (following Rabassa's interpretation) could only do so with plenty of "cultural baggage" attached. Precisely because Kafka wrote his story so as not to include details that would allow positive identification of the insect depicted, Kafka's protagonist in *The Metamorphosis* seems likely to be even further metamorphosed with every knew translation due to the fact that insects are not conceptualized in the same way from culture to culture.

Grammatical Differences from Language to Language

When culture-specific features of categorization are inextricably woven into the grammar of a language and thereby influence conceptualization (cf. Feldman 2006: 191), translators are forced to make difficult choices, the results of which may echo through the target text. For example, *potamos* (river) in Greek is a masculine noun but the gender of the Slavic *re&ka* is feminine (Jakobson 1959: 434). This being the case, I would venture that the respective translators of Ariyoshi's novel *Ki no kawa* (*The River Ki*), depicting the lives of three generations of Japanese women living along the river, would encounter some interfering nuances in Greek that would not be evident in Slavic.

Japanese nouns are not conceptualized according to gender but the system for counting plural nouns is significantly different from English. Whereas in English one specifies "one book" and uses a cardinal number in combination with the plural "books" for each quantitative increase thereafter, Japanese requires the use of many counting words that combine in complex ways with numbers to create grammatically complex plurals. The way that certain counters are paired with certain nouns in Japanese is similar to the way English allows one to say "a flock of sheep" but not "a gaggle of cows."

In that the Japanese noun for cow (*ushi*) is counted using a counting word that means "head" (*tō*), there are occasional moments of felicitous correspondence. For example, the phrase "*ushi santō*" can be translated perfectly as "3 head of cattle," after which the translator is likely to experience a moment of perplexed satisfaction. English precludes the expression "one head of cattle," however, so all permutations do not perform equally well even in the rare instances where conceptualization corresponds.

Japanese counting words do not simply repeat the noun or offer a different version of it to accomplish their function, they actually evoke a certain aspect of the noun's appearance or some other perceptible feature. For example, "one pencil" is expressed as "*enpitsu ippon*" (pencil one-ʻcylinderʼ) and "two cars" is expressed as "*kuruma nidai*" (car two-ʻplatformsʼ). While most of the pencils one is likely to encounter will indeed be cylindrical and most cars do involve riding in seats fastened onto a sort of moving platform, these specific aspects may not seem to be essential features to native speakers of English. The fact that these subtle aspects are foregrounded in Japanese leads to two specific effects, one effect occurring in Japanese to English translation and its inverse effect in English to Japanese. On one hand, semantic content will be lost when translating from Japanese to English. On the other, slight nuances, completely absent in the original, will be added when going from English to Japanese. The next section will detail a few ways that source and target texts semantically diverge due to differences in grammar and conceptualization between the two languages.

Source and Target Text Divergence as Semantic Difference

Whether the type of loss just described happens or not may be incidental in an everyday communication context, but when translating a literary work from one language (which uses counters) to another (which does not use them) the source text and target text may "diverge" in a more crucial way. Because repetition leads to instantiation in long-term memory (see chapter 4 for details), when such seemingly minor differences are repeated throughout a text the effect on conceptualization will increase to the extent that repetitions occur. If the feature displaying grammatical or conceptual difference happens to be linked to a central thematic component that is repeated often over an extended section of narrative, the gained or lost semantic value will at the very least "accrete," if not "compound."

Tabakowska notes how Polish authors strategically use pervasive diminutives (absent in English) to accomplish certain semantic effects. Through repetition, they are able to subtly control nuances of depiction either in a positive sense (i.e. "small and lovable") or a negative sense (i.e. "small and of poor quality") (Tabakowska 1993: 100-117). If the language that the translator is using prevents such a strategy, a low-profile yet relatively important semantic aspect of the text will be lost in translation.

Another example is evident in the Japanese translation (Kipling 1995) of Rudyard Kipling's short story, "The Bridge-Builders" (Kipling 1898). In a previous paper, I have asserted that the bridge depicted in the story is the work's major thematic element (Strack 2006a). In fact, the word "bridge," either standing alone or in conjunction with other words (as in "bridge-builder") is mentioned 65 times in the story's 33 pages for an average of 1.97 tokens per page. The total word count for the story is 12,582 words and so the ratio of bridge tokens to total words comes to 0.00516. When pronouns and other implicit references to bridges (i.e. synonyms like "arch," pronouns like "it" or terms that refer to specific parts of a bridge like "pier") are included, the total number of bridge references climbs to 205 for an average of 6.21 references per page.

Explicit bridge tokens and bridge placeholder tokens are very profuse within the source text.

In fact, "bridges" in the story are not simply profuse. In that the specific "bridge-builders" depicted in the story are building a bridge in India as an infrastructural project that is explicitly designed to benefit the British Empire, these characters are not simply "bridge-builders" in an engineering sense, but are also imperialistic "bridge-builders," creating the connections between Great Britain and India necessary to advance the Empire (cf. Strack 2006a). Kipling uses crucial details in his depiction of bridges to elucidate this metaphorical aspect unique to the context of the story. For this reason, bridges are profuse in the story not simply because Kipling happened to write a story about bridges; conversely, Kipling, in writing a story about imperialism, used the bridge metaphorically to instantiate a hidden level of commentary into the text.

This story is a prime example of diffused-domain extended metaphor. Extrapolating from the metaphor EMPIRE-BUILDERS ARE BRIDGE-BUILDERS, Kipling embeds implicit commentary concerning the underspecified domain of the story (EMPIRE-BUILDERS) into the explicit depiction of the concrete domain (BRIDGE-BUILDERS). This strategy allows Kipling to offer his opinions concerning the nature of imperialism in a way that is not didactic. He seems not to be explaining the nature of imperialism, only telling a story that happens to depict many details of bridge construction. This metaphorical depiction strategy does not rely on compact, single-sentence type metaphor. The two metaphorical domains are camouflaged in that they are both metonymically diffused throughout the narrative. Nevertheless, authors do tend to instantiate a few key passages that more or less explicitly link up the two domains. Kipling's story is no exception to this trend, as will be explained in chapter 8.

If "bridges" are indeed a key thematic element in the story, then differences in conceptualization between English and Japanese have the potential to greatly affect the efficacy of this diffused-domain metaphor in the Japanese translation. Has such a divergence (with potentially great impact on the story's overall metaphorical profile) occurred?

Hashimoto's translation, "*Hashi wo tsukuru mono tachi*" (Kipling 1995), runs 52 pages and I have estimated it to have around 29,800 characters. The Japanese character for "bridge" (橋) is used 103 times in the story for an average of 1.98 tokens per page. While this ratio seems to be an almost exact match for the original English text, the result is deceptive because the Japanese version runs 19 pages longer than its English counterpart. From this data we realize that the Japanese text refers to the *kanji* for bridge, *hashi* (橋), 103 times compared to the original English text's 65 references for the token "bridge," a difference of 38 tokens. Why has there been such a great divergence?

Close examination of the Japanese translation reveals a few factors that account for this difference. The most significant factor lies in the level of specificity of terms used to evoke the same concepts in the different languages. While Kipling's English text uses the word "pier" to indicate the pillars that support the body of the bridge and elevate it beyond the river's water level, the Japanese counterpart term is *kyōkyaku* (橋脚; literally, "bridge leg"). In that this common Japanese term for "pier" includes the Chinese character for bridge, already we have accounted for a 17-token increase in references to the word bridge. In 17 cases out of the 23 times a pier is mentioned in Kipling's original text, the Japanese translator has characterized it as *kyōkyaku* in Japanese. How might this particular change affect the story's semantic profile? (In the other 6 cases, the "pier" reference has either been elided or replaced with a pronoun.)

The extensive use of the Chinese character *kyaku* (leg) is likely to subtly amplify the anthropomorphic interpretation of the bridge already present in the story. Of course the type of anthropomorphism chosen by Kipling and that naturally occurring in Japanese does not usually match. For example, in the key scene in which a metaphorical battle between Mother Gunga (the Ganges River) and the bridge is described, we find the following anthropomorphized depiction:

Example 5.2

And they looked and wondered afresh at the deep water, the racing
water that <u>licked the throat of the piers</u>. (Kipling 1898 (1987): 16)

Translation 5.2

彼らは川の水の深さにあらためて驚いた。逆巻く水
が<u>橋脚の下を洗っていた</u>。(Kipling 1995: 150)

*Karera wa kawa no mizu no fukasa ni aratamete odoroita. Sakamaku mizu
ga <u>kyōkyaku no shita wo aratteita</u>.*

In the English expression "licked the throat of the piers," both the river (Mother
Gunga) and the bridge are described in terms of human (or possibly animal?)
bodily actions ("licking") or body parts ("throat"). In contrast to this relatively
foregrounded characterization in the original English, the Japanese translation
expresses the same phrase as "*kyōkyaku no shita wo aratteita*" which literally
means, "washed the lower part of the bridge-leg." In this case, Kipling's strong
anthropomorphism ("licked") has been minimized ("washed") and the word pier
has been expressed in terms of conventionalized anthropomorphism that
Japanese readers will not likely even notice as anthropomorphism. It seems that
the low-profile but consistent presence of the Japanese word for pier, "*kyō
kyaku*," in the translation, increases the likelihood that more foregrounded types
of anthropomorphism instantiated into the original depiction of the bridge will
go unnoticed by the reader even in cases when the author attempts to translate
them.

In contrast, the anthropomorphized depiction of the Ganges River as
"Mother Gunga" is more consistently foregrounded in the translation just as it
was in the source text. In the final analysis, idiosyncrasies relating to the way
that the word "pier" is translated into Japanese (along with the translator's tendency to replace strong anthropomorphic metaphors with mundane and less

noticeable ones) have resulted in an overall diminishment of anthropomorphic characterization of the bridge in the story. While the main metaphorical formulation of the story remains intact, one aspect of the formulation, namely the adversarial relationship between traditional India and the imperialists as implied by the anthropomorphized battle between Mother Gunga and the bridge, has also been diminished.

Differing idiosyncrasies of conceptualization and subsequent textual divergence aside, the fact remains that explicit references to the bridges are generally retained in Hashimoto's translation. For this reason, diffused-domain metaphor is unlikely to be completely eliminated from a text as a result of translation. To the extent that elements of a diffused-domain metaphor are (as its name indicates) diffused throughout the text, a few specific instances in which the metaphorical aspects are elided or otherwise diminished are unlikely to effect the overall metaphorical pattern. Nevertheless, diffused-domain metaphor will be more likely to survive according to the extent to which domain elements are profuse within the text.

On the Cross-cultural Viability of Japanese Aesthetic Concepts

The history of Japanese literature is replete with terms that very subtly differentiate aesthetic atmospheres. For example, the term *yūgen* (very roughly translated as "mysterious profundity") has been used to describe certain types of remote, slightly dark, and sometimes Buddhist-inspired atmospheres in *waka* and other types of Japanese poetry since at least 905 A.D. (Watanabe 1992: 1710). Over a millennium, the term evolved and was reinterpreted often enough that, in the 21st century, thorough attempts to explain it would require a full chapter or perhaps even an entire book.

In his research on Japanese *Haiku* and translation, Dr. Jun'ichiro Takachi has focused on two aesthetic categories, 風流 (*fūryū*) and 風雅 (*fūga*). According to Takachi, "*Fūryū*-mind" [風流] is an element central to poet

Matsuo Bashō's conception of *haiku* (Takachi 2004). "*Fūga*-spirit" ［風雅］ represents Bashō's lofty aesthetic understanding while *Fūryū* represents the stylistic aspects of his thought that he imparted to his disciples. Takachi contends that "*Fūryū*-mind" cannot be understood apart from an understanding of Bashō and his oeuvre. For this reason, he has strong opinions concerning attempts to translate the following *haiku* by Bashō (Matsuo 1976: 105):

Poem 5.1

風流のはじめや奥の田植うた

fūryū no hajime ya oku no ta-ue uta

In this *haiku, oku* refers to the "interior" area of Japan that Bashō visited on his 1689 journey through the Tō-hoku and Hokuriku regions. *Hajime* means "the beginning of something," *ta-ue* is "rice planting," and *uta* means "song" or sometimes "poem." *No* (used twice in the *haiku*) is a common Japanese possessive and *ya* is an example of *kireji* (a "cutting word"). While the word *oku* is also extremely evocative in indicating both the name of an inner area, "*Michi-n'oku*", and the "heart of human nature" at the same time, the more perplexing problem is that, according to Takachi, there can be no translation of *fūryū* into English that does not do gross injustice to the subtlety of the concept, a concept central to Bashō's poetic artistry. To emphasize its importance, Takachi's translation (Takachi 2004) of Poem 5.1 reads as follows:

Translation 5.3

It's the real beginning
Of *Fūryū*—a rice-planting song
Here in the inland

By leaving the term *fūryū* untouched, Takachi offers the reader a new aesthet-

WHEN WORLDS COLLIDE *99*

ic concept to consider, a concept that can only be grasped through intensive study of Bashō and his ancestral spirits. The only hope the reader has of understanding *fūryū* is to become one of Bashō's disciples.

There are many other Japanese "atmospheric" terms that do not translate well into English. A few more examples might include *yūga* ("gentle and refined") and its corollary term *miyabi* ("elegantly sophisticated"), *ūshin* ("poignant") and the related but slightly different critical appraisal *kororo ari* ("essential" or "humane"). While I have included simple definitions for basic reference, in fact, none of these literary values can be straightforwardly defined without great loss since each carries with it the weight of countless literary associations with poets and critics going back, in some cases, more than one-thousand years. To attempt to thoroughly recreate such historically embedded Japanese poetic aesthetic concepts for the benefit of a modern-day non-Japanese reader is a hopeless task.

Having said this, even with respect to the original text, one could not expect any but the most scholarly modern Japanese readers to comprehend the ancient aesthetic nuances in the same way that the poets of the respective time period (and some of their disciples) would have. Interlingual failures in communication that result from translation must be weighed against failures in communication generally among people of the same culture, which often slip by undetected. Steiner remarks, "[o]n the inter-lingual level, translation will pose concentrated, visibly intractable problems; but these same problems abound, at a more covert or conventionally neglected level, intra-lingually" (Steiner 1998: 47). The expectation for a perfect translation of a text's "original meaning" is based on the false assumption that the source text afforded some sort of perfect communication; perfect communication does not exist even when both speaker and listener are using the same language. Especially in the case of ancient texts, the group of ideal readers the author envisioned while writing the poem is long gone but even they may not have understood all of what the author was attempting to communicate.

When readers don't understand some aspect of a work by a famous author in the original language, the responsibility for failed communication can easily be pinned on the reader. When the same thing happens within a work in translation, however, translators are more likely to shoulder the blame. Perhaps this is an inevitable result of accepting a literary "canon" (of any type) in which authors are deified and works are thus seen as sacred texts. According to this "sacred canon" metaphor, translators are like priests who bear the heavy responsibility of bringing about the consubstantiation of the communion elements and proffering them to the faithful communicants without spilling a drop or losing a crumb.

Poem 5.2

Excerpt from *Take* by Hagiwara Sakutarō (1917b: 21-22; Strack Translation)

竹	*Take*
光る地面に竹が生え、	*Hikaru jimen ni take ga hae,*
青竹が生え、	*aodake ga hae,*
地下には竹の根が生え、	*chika ni wa take no ne ga hae,*
根がしだいにほそらみ、	*ne ga shidai ni hosorami,*
根の先より繊毛が生え、	*ne no saki yori senmō ga hae,*
かすかにけぶる繊毛が生え、	*kasuka ni keburu senmō ga hae,*
かすかにふるえ。	*kasuka ni furue.*
かたき地面に竹が生え、	*Kataki jimen ni take ga hae,*
地上にするどく竹が生え、	*chijō ni surudoku take ga hae,*
まっしぐらに竹が生え、	*masshigura ni take ga hae,*
凍れる節節りんりんと	*kōreru fushi-bushi rin-rin to,*
青空のもとに竹が生え、	*aozora no moto ni take ga hae,*

竹、竹、竹が生え。　　　　　　*take, take, take ga hae.*

Bamboo

In the bright ground, bamboo is growing

green bamboo is growing

under the ground, bamboo roots are growing

roots extending, gradually narrowing

from the root tips, fibers are growing

softly, a cloud of fibers is growing

softly, trembling

Up from the hard ground, bamboo is growing

above the ground, pointed bamboo is growing

straight up, bamboo is growing

frozen, joint upon joint, echoing boldly

beneath the blue sky, bamboo is growing

bamboo, bamboo, bamboo is growing

Iconicity Disrupted

In the 13 lines of Poem 5.2, Hagiwara Sakutarō's free-verse poem *Take* (Hagiwara 1917b: 21-22), the phrase *take ga hae* ("bamboo grows") repeats 7 times and the word *take* (bamboo) repeats 10 times with 3 of these instances occurring in the final line alone. This staccato repetition of hard consonants, especially the final "*take, take, take ga hae*" creates a strong, uncompromising image of the plant. The word "bamboo," in contrast, sounds 'resilient,' with not a hint of the original poem's hard-edged consonants. To compound the problem, bamboo is not found at all in the United Kingdom and is relatively rare in North America so English speakers from these and perhaps other areas may not have a clear awareness of what a bamboo plant is actually like. While capturing the poem's basic meaning is not an impossibility and although some similar aural effects can certainly be achieved, the poem, which depicts a *take* plant struggling up through the cold, hard earth to grow straight and tall is an image that the bobbing, bubbling, bumbling word "bamboo" in English has nothing whatsoever to do with.

Bergen, in his 2004 paper, "The Psychological Reality of Phonaesthemes," notes that the key property of phoaesthemes is that they manifest the recurrent pairing of "formal and semantic properties of words." In the study, he examines words that display a consistency of morphological and semantic similarity in the lexicon (like *glimmer, glisten, glitter*, and *gleam*) and concludes that "when a form-meaning pairing recurs sufficiently often, it comes to take on priming behavior that cannot be explained as the result of form or meaning priming, alone or in combination" (Bergen 2004: 307). In other words, humans have an ability to sense and react to subtle statistical associations that are present in their lexicon and thereby collectively reinforce them.

Translators, when faced with the task of translating the Japanese *take* into English as "bamboo" face a dilemma resulting from the differing phonaesthemic associations of the words bamboo and *take*. Only two options are available to the translator: either use the English "bamboo" and change the poem's atmosphere due to the subtle influence of these phonaesthemic associations or use the Romanization of *take* in the translation itself. If the second course were to be taken, it would probably be better to avoid using unsightly footnotes. Exactly what would a translation making use of such transliteration be like? Translation 5.4 provides one possible example.

Translation 5.4

A Revised Translation of the Excerpt from *Take* by Hagiwara Sakutarō
(1917b: 21-22; Strack Translation)

Take (Bamboo)

In the bright ground, *take* is growing

green *take* is growing

under the ground, *take* roots are growing

roots extending, gradually narrowing

from the root tips, fibers are growing

softly, a cloud of fibers is growing

softly, trembling

Up from the hard ground, *take* is growing

above the ground, pointed *take* is growing

straight up, *take* is growing

frozen, joint upon joint, echoing boldly

beneath the blue sky, take is growing

take, take, take is growing

Reading through Translation 5.4, the native English-speaking reader may have noticed that the word "*take*" can easily be mistaken for the English word, "take." Perhaps transliterating it as *také* might solve the problem. It becomes evident that neither using the phonaesthemically unfortunate "bamboo" nor using "*take*" with its *faux* English spelling are completely satisfactory. Once again, the translator must think back upon the goals of translation, negotiate among the various options available, and finally, sadly, compromise.

Translation scholar Tabakowska has asserted that "all texts are translatable in so far as they are interpretable" (Tabakowska 1993: 77). Doubts about this statement begin to arise when considering literary texts such as Hagiwara's free-verse poem *Take* in which what must be "interpreted" is not merely semantic or formal but a combination of the two. As I have demonstrated in the preceding passage, and as Hiraga has demonstrated in great detail throughout her book on literary iconicity (Hiraga 2005), formal aspects of literary works are often interpretable not only as perceptible effects but simultaneously as indicators of underlying semantic artifice. Often these formal effects do not function in a single mode but serve to highlight corresponding semantic aspects that are also interpretable.

Although the example *Take* (Poem 5.2) above clearly represents a difficult case, it is not clear to me that a translation of the poem is destined to be an unmitigated failure. As has been detailed, various compromises are possible and, of course, each compromise is bound to result in some sort of literary, cultural, or linguistic change. Nevertheless, depending on the goals of the translator and the intercultural and interlinguistic idiosyncrasies *of the specific text*, translation at a high level of analogous meaning accompanied by analogous form that highlights that meaning may, in fact, be possible.

In translating a literary work, will the results be less unified in the effects they achieve when compared with the original work? It seems likely. Is translation then irrelevant because it cannot perfectly live up to the original work in every way simultaneously? Only if the goal is perfection. For translators whose goal is perfection and will not be satisfied with anything less, for uncompromising perfectionists (including most poets), the translation of poetry will be a lost cause. For the remaining translators, however, for those who may be perfectionists at heart but nevertheless concentrate on more attainable goals than lofty-sounding but ultimately chimeric perfection, the translation of poetry is certainly possible. Much depends on expectations.

The Problem of Background Knowledge

In Guy de Maupassant's short story, "*Apparition*" (Maupassant 1987a), the setting for an old gentleman's telling of a ghost story is an old family mansion located on the "rue de Grenelle." In the English translation (Maupassant 2002: 112), this street name is expressed simply as "Rue de Grenelle," apparently assuming that the reader of the English translation will have sufficient knowledge of French and French culture to realize that it is the name of a street in Paris. Perhaps not coincidentally, the story's Japanese translator, Okamoto Kidō, as well, transliterates the street name as "*rū do gureneru*" (Maupassant 1987b). When I first read the story I did not know the meaning of the word "rue" and it bothered me that the translator would assume I would know it. It seems unfair to leave certain French words untranslated when the translation has presumably been prepared for a reader with little or no knowledge of French. Does the translator expect the reader to keep an interlingual dictionary at hand during reading?

Such problems associated with background knowledge are, to some extent, related to the issue of narrative framing with reference to a translation's likely readership. Weise has noted that when a translator has an understanding of the level of relevant knowledge readers possess and when the text is relatively balanced to reader competence, comprehension is facilitated (Weise 1994: 100, 104). While the translators of scientific and medical texts may estimate the extent of their likely readers' knowledge based on estimates related to the specific field of research to be translated (Scarpa 2002: 146), the broad range of potential readers of literature in translation makes this problematic.

The problem is more acute for literary works translated into English than those translated into Japanese. Works translated into Japanese still include an implicit assumption that the works are primarily, if not entirely, intended for native speakers of Japanese to read. This is clearly not the case with English at present. Just as Hollywood motion pictures have learned to cater to an international audience, so literature both written in English and translated from other languages into English can no longer rely on a predominantly native English speaking readership.

When translating a literary text, the translator should ideally have or have access to a number of "knowledge sets." Of course no translator's knowledge will be perfect, but without a certain level of knowledge, the translation will likely include amateurish mistakes, will lack coherence, and, worst of all, may cause the reader to doubt the skills of the translator. In most cases, readers read the translation to understand the work and the author and assume that the translator will skillfully give them access to these. Once the trust relationship with the translator comes into question, the reader will begin to read critically, looking for more mistakes, perhaps finding them even where they do not exist, and may even lose sight of the work itself.

For this reason, it is important to have a knowledge of one's own blind spots and to know "what [one] does not know" (Steiner 1998: 412). Awareness of the gaps in one's own knowledge base will both spur the translator to study problematic areas in depth so as to avoid obvious factual mistakes or, less ideally, at least to make the translator aware that phrasing may need to be adjusted so as to rhetorically disguise this lack of knowledge. In any case, overconfidence concerning areas in which the translator's background knowledge is minimal can result in glaring mistakes that risk alienating knowledgeable readers.

Translators must not only fill in their own cultural and linguistic blindspots before proceeding with translation, but once they have become sufficiently knowledgeable, they must then judge who the prospective readers of their translation will be and what knowledge base they will have. Should one write "up" to the level of the Anglophone who has visited or lived in Paris but does not speak much French or "write down" to the reader who thinks "rue" means to regret? The answer, as mentioned before, will flow naturally from what the translator hopes to accomplish by translating the work.

In a sense, this need to find the right balance between accommodating one's readers and spurring them toward a new understanding of the target language and culture echoes the conflict faced by the literary author in composition. Booth explains the conflict in the following way:

> The author makes his readers. If he makes them badly — that is, if he simply waits, in all purity, for the occasional reader whose perceptions and norms happen to match his own, then his conception must be lofty indeed if we are to forgive him for his bad craftsmanship. But if he makes them well — that is, makes them see what they have never seen before, moves them into a new order of perception and experience altogether — he finds his reward in the peers he has created. (Booth 1961: 397-398)

Perhaps the first task for the translator, then, should be to discover what she hopes to accomplish through the translation. Does she hope to push the envelope of linguistic orthodoxy in the target language and thereby promote the culture of the text's origin? Does she hope to promote the author, or a certain viewpoint? Is there an aesthetic aspect worth expressing, one that will not only pique interest in sensual terms but also abstractly mirror some associational resonance in the text? To answer the complex questions posed by translation without first determining one's own viewpoint on the work increases the possibility of producing a translation that cannot live up to the translator's own expectations.

6

THE SQUEAKY WHEEL

By "minor poems" I mean, of course, poems of little length. And here, in the beginning, permit me to say a few words in regard to a somewhat peculiar principle, which, whether rightfully or wrongfully, has always had its influence in my own critical estimate of the poem. I hold that a long poem does not exist. I maintain that the phrase, "a long poem," is simply a flat contradiction in terms.

   I need scarcely observe that a poem deserves its title only inasmuch as it excites, by elevating the soul. The value of the poem is in ratio of this elevating excitement. But all excitements are, through a psychal necessity, transient. That degree of excitement which would entitle a poem to be so called at all, cannot be sustained throughout a composition of any great length.

Edgar Allan Poe

(1850: 228)

Although writing long before the age of neuroscience, Edgar Allan Poe was at least fundamentally correct in pointing out the fact that "psychal" effects cannot be sustained for long. A keen critic, Poe goes on to note how Milton's *Paradise Lost*, although seeming to be an exception to his newly stated principle, in fact, is not. He observes that the effect of *Paradise Lost* is uneven because it would be impossible to maintain the level of enthusiasm typically associated with the reading of poetry throughout: "If, to preserve its Unity — its totality of effect or impression — we read it (as would be necessary) at a single sitting, the result is but a constant alternation of excitement and depression" (Poe 1850: 228-229).

Stockwell, also making reference to Milton, notes that "[a]ttention is basically selective, which means that the ground at any given point in a literary reading is deselected, or characterized by *neglect*. Attention given to the figure will necessarily involve less attention being paid to other elements" (Stockwell 2002: 87). To the extent that active elements are naturally foregrounded in attention, conversely, elements that are static, inactive, or (I would assert) unusually repetitious, become part of the background.

Indeed, Poe's description of *Paradise Lost* above fits in perfectly with Stockwell's insight. To the extent that the meter of *Paradise Lost* contrasts with whatever language the reader has experienced before sitting down to read, it will be foregrounded at the outset. Because the reading takes such a long time to complete, however, the reader gradually becomes desensitized to the meter because it is a "static" (that is to say extremely repetitious and therefore predictable) element. Poe was correct in just this sense. When foregrounded auditory (or some other type of attention-getting) phenomena are gradually pushed into the background through desensitization, the text must find some other way to engage the reader's cognition.

Stockwell's analysis of one of Milton's sonnets goes on to describe effects that have strong conceptual elements, including depiction of physical activity and words that relate to visual stimuli. These become prominent "attractors" one after another as the reader proceeds (Stockwell 2002: 87-89). Milton seems to have a number of "attractive" strategies for keeping the reader's attention occupied after the neural apparatus of auditory perception has been temporarily put out of action. This is not to say that auditory attention-getting effects will not subsequently reappear. Poe implies that they do when he mentions "alternation of excitement and depression" (Poe 1850: 228). Such a viewpoint is consistent with van Peer's (1986) characterizations of how stylistic patterns garner reader attention and thereby cause foregrounded elements to (temporarily) recede while background elements (temporarily) become more prominent. As such, longer works cannot afford to allow a single aesthetic value to dominate. They must offer alternatives.

The Translator as Reader

When singer/songwriter James Taylor observed that the "squeaky wheel [is] always getting the grease" (Taylor 1976), he was not referring to translation but he might as well have been. If one were to ask translators about the criteria they use for selecting aspects of a given text to emphasize in translation, I suspect that, upon reflection, most would respond that they merely translate the aspects they notice.

So then, what are the aspects they notice? In many cases the aspects they notice will be the same aspects that readers in general notice. "Noticed" aspects may be characterized as those that break the surface of consciousness during reading, with some aspects being temporarily foregrounded and then receding, only to be replaced by other aspects. This roller-coaster ride of attention cannot help but affect the ultimate results of translation.

To the extent that a translator translates as she reads, without careful analysis or time for measured contemplation of the work, what kind of results will be forthcoming? A translator who notices things and then attempts to translate the most noticeable effects into the target language may succeed in selecting the more prominent effects overall, thereby effectively "de-selecting" the less prominent. In this way, translation will proceed quickly and effortlessly toward a final product, relying on the moment-to-moment noticing skills of the translator.

Deciding which effects to translate based on real-time intuitions during reading is akin to the "triaging" of wounded soldiers done by medical personnel in wartime, a process in which those with minor injuries and severe but survivable wounds are separated off from those who seem likely to die. After the decisions have been made, there will be no time to reconsider those who have been written off. Without time for fine distinctions, quick judgments are made that result in outcomes that are acceptable given the dire circumstances of war but which would be unacceptable otherwise.

While time pressure is not unknown to translators and so there may indeed be reasons for working quickly, translating a literary work using only information from moment to moment perception during a single reading can only result in damage to the work, with more sophisticated and complex works being damaged to a greater extent. When auditory effects are predominant, associational elements go unnoticed. When the auditory effects thereafter begin to fade due to neural resource depletion and desensitization, then associational elements will become relatively more prominent. Exactly when these fade-ins and fade-outs will occur for the individual translator may be quite unpredictable. The results of translation may be determined by whether the translator has gotten enough sleep the previous night or not.

A further problem results from such an approach because, as already explained in chapter 4, in many cases the grammatical, visual, or auditory phenomena that attract the reader's attention are not stand-alone effects but actually function as access points to important conceptual aspects of the text. Many of the patterns perceived in literary works are noticed as patterns precisely because authors hope they will be noticed and thereby lead the reader to corresponding conceptual patterns. For illustration, please refer to Examples 6.1 and 6.2.

Example 6.1

Vedi Napoli, e poi muori.

(See Naples and die.)

Example 6.2

日光を見ずして結構と言うなかれ

Nikkō wo mizu shite kekkō to iu nakare

(You haven't seen it all till you've seen Nikkō)

These "proverbs" are less proverbs than examples of slogans advocating local tourism. Relating specifically to Naples, Italy, and Nikkō, Tochigi Prefecture, Japan, they are similar not just in their propaganda value. Both of these proverbs display parallelism in their structure that emphasizes auditory similarities between the first and second halves of each statement. In Example 6.1, both "*vedi*" and "*e poi*" as well as "*Napoli*" and "*muori*" are (imperfectly) rhymed. In Example 6.2, the predominant sonic similarity is between "*Nikkō*" and "*kekkō*," both of these including a sharp glottal stop before the identical "kō" at the end of each word.

What is the point of instantiating such strong, succinct, easily remembered auditory phenomena into what amounts to a verbal travel brochure? One does not need to be an advertising executive to know the answer. The auditory effects that have been included serve to leverage attention and turn the saying into a kind of "verbal virus" that hearers will unwittingly contract. If an interesting combination of auditory effects can enable the most banal of advertisements to become consolidated in long-term memory upon a single hearing, all the better. Chances that the perceiver of the foregrounded auditory phenomena will notice it undoubtedly increase the likelihood that they will remember it, occasionally repeat it aloud at the mere mention of each city's name, and visit Naples or Nikkō at some point in the future. Such strategies are not limited to auditory phenomena, as evidenced by the effectively foregrounded English-language logograph in the tourism-promoting slogan: "I ♡ New York!"

Parallelisms found in poetry often have grammatical, visual, and auditory elements that elicit attention not simply because the author desires to instantiate a parallelism on the form plane but because language is the surest way to ignite the fireworks of conceptual activity in a coordinated fashion. For this reason, it may not be enough for a translator to simply take note of some formal effects "evident" in the text and attempt to achieve similar formal effects in the target language. Precisely because attention and conceptualization have been blended in the text it is necessary to notice how they interact. Does some consistently repetitive auditory effect point to a recurring conceptual theme? Does the visual pairing of stanzas on the printed page reflect a conceptual pairing of ideas central to understanding the work? Is the foregrounded accent or regional dialect of a protagonist meant to set the speaker apart from other characters being depicted? In the next section, I will explain how highlighted aspects of dialogue subtly attract attention in prose works.

Foregrounded Aspects of Dialogue in Literature

Miyamoto Teru and Ariyoshi Sawako are two Japanese novelists that make skillful use of regional dialects in their fictional works. This is not to imply that their works are written entirely in Ōsaka-ben or Kishū-ben. In fact the narrators of, for example, Miyamoto's Doro no kawa (1978) and Ariyoshi's Ki no kawa (1959) narrate the stories in standard (generally speaking, Tokyo) Japanese. If they hope to use local dialects from the Kansai region, why haven't they simply narrated their novels entirely in dialect? It seems likely that they had in mind the fact that a great many of their readers would not be from the Kansai region and so, although characters depicted as living in Osaka or Wakayama would be expected to speak in their local dialects for the sake of authenticity, the narrator need not. Does the explanation end here? The translator cannot assume that it does.

In such cases, the reader quickly perceives a discrepancy between the language used in the dialogue and the standard Japanese of the narrator. For example, Ki no kawa contains the short dialogue in Example 6.3 (Ariyoshi 1959:

19). A character named Hana has asked a character named Toku to open a door.

Example 6.3

「これでよろしゅございますかのし」
「おおきに」

   "Kore de yoroshu gozaimasu ka no shi"
   "Ōki ni"

In Example 6.3, the typical Japanese expressions used in everyday situations, *"Kore de yoroshī desu ka ne"* (This is okay, isn't it?; cf. *"Kishū ben"*) and *"Arigatō"* (Thank you), are replaced by Kansai dialect equivalents. While the expression of casual conversation in local dialect adds atmosphere to the story and can even make something as mundane as a request to open a door sound more interesting, the use of dialect also serves to create variation in the narrative so as to heighten interest. As the language used vacillates between the standard Japanese of the narrator and the local dialect of the protagonists, readers find interest in the contrasting vocabulary and communication styles that will not be evident in a novel written entirely in standard Japanese. It may be that the author, in incorporating such a back and forth "dialectic" strategy, hopes not only to add interest but actually to imply that, to the degree that the speaking styles of characters in the story differ from the Japanese mainstream, their values and attitudes do, as well.

      Unfortunately, there is no natural way to translate these dialectic differences because the linguistic and cultural differences between standard Japanese and those of regional dialects cannot be precisely recreated in a foreign language. Of course the tension sometimes evident when city-dwellers and country-folk get together is a relatively universal phenomenon. In the American context, then, the comments of a Tokyoite might be expressed using words appropriate to a New Yorker, while someone from a rural area of Japan might be given a dialect from, for example, Mississippi.

This is precisely the strategy employed by William Faulkner's Italian translator. According to Eco, "Pavese had turned to Piedmontese dialect for translating certain passages in Faulkner" (Eco 2004: 266) so as to write the foregrounded dialogue in Italian but only after having "rinsed it in the Mississippi." Eco's comment reveals the potential for such transformed dialects to bring along with them associations never imagined by the original author.

While the city and countryside distinction may be useful in some cases, what about the language differences apparent between Tokyo-dwellers and residents of Osaka, another very large city located in a different part of Japan? Is it the difference between New York and Newark, New Jersey? Between New York and Boston? Between New York and Chicago? And, in the end, even if the translator could find a target-culture approximation of the cultural tension evident in the Tokyo-Osaka intercity relationship, would there be a great enough disparity in linguistic expression to allow the reader to consistently notice the difference, as is the case with Japanese? Most such dialect differences are, although very noticeable in context, untranslatable, which is why the English translations of *Doro no kawa* (*River of Mud*; Miyamoto 1991) and *Ki no kawa* (*The River Ki*; Ariyoshi 1981) make no consistent attempts to interpolate dialect-based effects.

F. Scott Fitzgerald's short story "May Day" (1920), with its wide range of characters depicted, offers a number of intriguing juxtapositions of disparate verbal styles. In one scene, an "uptown" sophisticate who has been drinking too much at a Yale reunion party encounters two "downtowners" (recently released from military service) who have been hiding in a hotel broom closet while waiting for their chance to steal some alcohol from the party. A language-circumscribed "intercultural" encounter ensues:

116

Example 6.4

Peter bowed.

"How do you do?" he said.

Private Rose set one foot slightly in front of the other, poised for fight, flight, or compromise.

"How do you do?" repeated Peter politely.

"I'm o'right." (Fitzgerald 1920: 120)

Translation 6.1

ピーターがお辞儀をして言った。

「こんにちは、ごきげんいかがですか？」

ローズ一等兵は片足をわずかに前に出し、戦闘、退却、講和、いずれの

行動にも移れる態勢をとった。

「ごきげんいかが？」ピーターは丁重に繰り返す。

「ごきげんはまあまあってとこよ」 (Fitzgerald 1992a: 143)

Pītā ga o-jigi wo shite itta.

"Kon'nichiwa, go kigen ikaga desu ka?"

Rōzu ittohei wa kata'ashi wo wazuka ni mae ni dashi, sentō, taikyaku, kō-wa, izure no kōdō ni mo utsureru jōtai wo totta.

"Go-kigen ikaga?" Pītā wa teichō ni kurikaesu.

"Go-kigen wa māmā-tte toko yo"

What makes this passage rather difficult to translate is the way that Peter uses an intentionally ambiguous question to obliquely make fun of Rose, realizing that the Private will not likely know how to respond. If one interprets Peter's question "How do you do?" literally as "How are you?", then from a strictly semantic viewpoint, the response "I'm o'right" is a good match. Generally, however, the question does not function according to its literal meaning; it is often part of a conventionalized exchange upon meeting someone for the first time. If one

THE SQUEAKY WHEEL   *117*

interprets Peter's question to mean "nice to meet you," then "I'm o'right" is not such a good match.

Pragmatics aside, the marked disparity in politeness levels evident in the English text has been easily accommodated in Japanese. Peter's over-polite question "How do you do?" finds an equivalently foregrounded counterpart in the Japanese expression, "*Go-kigen wa ikaga desu ka*" (How is (your) (honorific-) mood?). A typical polite response to this question would be "*O-kage sama de.*" This conventional answer literally means, "thanks to you" with the implication being that the person is fine thanks to the good will or help of the questioner. Such a correct response, however, does not fit the situation described in the scene.

The question then is, how will Private Rose's brief and mildly inappropriate reply be handled in the translation? Sensing a chance to make the most of an already interesting passage, the translator Saeki perhaps overplays his hand by opting for the statement, "*Go-kigen wa māmā-tte toko yo,*" (literally, "(my)(honorific-)mood is okay at the moment (intensifier)." This response (like its English counterpart) does not offer an orthodox answer to the question "*Go-kigen wa ikaga desu ka,*" and furthermore, combines an incorrect use of the Japanese polite prefix "*go-*" (which cannot be used to refer to one's own mood) with inappropriately informal word choice, and two slang abbreviations ("*tokoro*" to "*toko*", and "*to iu*" to "*-tte*"). The answer is markedly inappropriate and even sounds somewhat inauthentic; that is, it would be hard to imagine a Japanese person seriously responding in such a way. While it is possible that the translator intended the phrase to seem intentionally impudent, this situation would not match Rose's noncommittal reply in English. Nevertheless, the response is more amusing in translation than Fitzgerald's understated original.

Private Rose's response in the original English is both inappropriate enough to be mildly amusing and succinct enough to convey the fact that Rose is not in any way showing undue respect to Peter through his choice of words.

The Japanese translation, on the other hand, by having Rose use the honorific prefix "go-" to inappropriately refer to himself, accentuates the humor at the expense of brevity. Nevertheless, the inappropriateness of Rose's reply in Japanese would have been foregrounded even without the misuse of the honorific.

In Fitzgerald's "May Day," there is a latent tension always present just below the surface of many of the dialogues. While the conversation at the hotel broom closet ends amicably as Peter offers the men a drink, the general mood of the scene seems to indicate that this was not an inevitable outcome. It could be said that the tension in the scene dissipates somewhat prematurely due to the relatively more humorous nature of Rose's response in the translation. In such a situation, is it better for the translator to play up the humorous aspects to add interest or attempt to strictly adhere to the carefully calibrated tension that builds to a violent outburst at the story's end? This question can only be answered by the individual translator with reference to specific goals for the text.

Earlier in the same scene, when the Yale graduate initially realizes that the two men are hiding in the closet, he looks in their direction and murmurs the expression "Peek-a-boo!" (Fitzgerald 1920: 120). The Japanese translation notes that Peter murmers "*inai inai bā*" (Fitzgerald 1992a: 142), a phrase used in Japanese to get the attention of infants. Comparing the two expressions, "Peek-a-boo!" and "*inai inai bā*," one is struck by how similar they are despite the obvious difference in culture of origin. Both English-speaking and Japanese-speaking adults have strictly formulated expressions for eliciting noticing from infants when showing one's face suddenly to them and, furthermore, these expressions both take advantage of the bobbing, bubbling, baby-attracting consonant "b." Wisely, the translator has not overlooked this very translatable correlation between US and Japanese "baby words."

Interest, Attention, and Translatability

While dialogues depicted in literary works differ somewhat in the ways they attempt to foreground regional dialects and social status of the speakers depicted, there is one commonality among them: the verbally instantiated discrepancies are interesting, and for this reason, attract attention. With respect to visual attention, research by O'Regan, Rensick, and Clark has shown that "[o]nly the parts of the environment that observers attend to and encode as interesting are available for making comparisons" (O'Regan et al. 1999: 34). This feature of visual perception undoubtedly has parallels in the reading process, as well. As attention determines neural resource allocation, things we find "interesting" will naturally procure more of the neural resources necessary for instantiation and consolidation.

Matter Mandler notes that "[e]ven when we are trying to memorize a [visual] scene, what we find uninteresting or ordinary may be attended but is processed so poorly that major changes to the boring bits often go unrecognized at a later time" (Matter Mandler 2004: 69). This tendency to attend to the obvious and neglect everything else will play a crucial role when aspects of dialogue are foregrounded in a literary text.

Because foregrounded dialect use (as in the stories by Ariyoshi and Miyamoto) adds interest for the reader, it will likely do so for the translator, as well. It has already been observed that it is extremely difficult to translate such dialect differences but the less obvious point is that because the dialect use attracts the translator's attention, it simultaneously distracts from whatever else might be in the text. As a result, the extremely interesting original work (with dialect use and other more subtle effects) tends to go completely "flat" in its translation (without the dialect use but *also without* the other more subtle effects).

In regard to the translation of dialogue that shows evidence of social stratification, it seems to be a relatively simple task to accomplish when translating from English to Japanese. This is no doubt due to the fact that Japanese is filled with subtle ways to express social stratification. American English has relatively fewer options available. For this reason, if a writer using American English succeeds in foregrounding disparities in social status in a text, the Japanese translator can accommodate these from an extremely large repertoire of options. On the other hand, when the American English-using translator is forced to translate the subtleties of Japanese hierarchical relationships into English, her failure is nearly assured because 21st century American English is such an unwieldy, broad brush to use for such fine detail work.

Due to the ways that readers and translators notice some aspects explicitly and notice others either implicitly or not at all, there is a tendency for the more noticeable effects to "escalate" as they are translated, while the more subtle effects disappear entirely. Furthermore, especially in situations where the two texts are compatible, the translator will be tempted to make the most of them. As these two factors work in combination, carefully calibrated effects in the original can skew toward "stylization" and "caricature," these coming at the expense of careful balance or understatement that may be evident in the original.

Such trends do not inevitably lead in a negative direction. It might be asserted that as amplification and intensification of effects occur in translation, certain works will become even more interesting than they were in the original language. This is no doubt one factor that can explain why literary works can be interesting in translation at all. If the original comprises the kind of literary values that will survive or even thrive in translation, then interlingual success becomes more likely. On the contrary, works that include effects (such as heavy emphasis on differences in dialect) that distract translators from other more translatable aspects are works that tend to fall flat.

On the Dual Risks of Under- and Over-analysis

Poet and critic Robert Conquest's observation that "[e]xplosively intended phrases tend to distract attention from any broader pattern" (Conquest 2004) may serve as a warning for the unwary translator. In the original work, broader patterns, although they may go unnoticed as the reader begins to read may nevertheless be discovered by the reader at a later time in a subsequent passage. Alternatively, the reader may go back to the text again and again, responding to the attraction of the more "explosive" patterns, until finally, becoming desensitized to such patterns, a different, never before recognized effect in the macrostructure suddenly appears. For this reason, translators that translate only what they find interesting in a complex text during the first or second reading are likely to miss broader, more subtle patterns.

On the other hand, there may be ambiguous or extremely subtle aspects of source texts that will fail to become transparent no matter how many times the translator reads the text. And in some cases, even if the translator identifies a subtle literary effect that might aid in a reader's appreciation of a text, the translator must make compromises. It could be asserted that such fine detail work does not lend itself to translation. In such cases, wouldn't it be better just to translate moment by moment using a "triage approach" and not worry about fine details that would probably end up getting left out anyway?

In all likelihood there will be texts that will be impervious to a translator's analysis or texts so complex that attempts to recreate every effect would be virtually precluded. One text that comes to mind is Spanish poet Federico García Lorca's poem, "*Ciudad sin Sueño* (*Nocturno del Brooklyn Bridge*)" (García Lorca 1987: 95-96). I once made an ill-advised attempt to translate this poem. After finishing, I read through the results and realized that my translation was mostly incomprehensible. Figuring that my limited knowledge of Spanish was to blame, I purchased an English translation (García Lorca 1990) of García Lorca's collection *Poeta en Nueva York* to compare with. Judging from the "authorized" translation, the results of my own translation had not been as far off as I had first suspected. It may be that this poem is quite translatable, but nevertheless resistant to analysis. The odd juxtapositioning of iguanas, crocodiles, and corpses, coupled with the sky and the Brooklyn Bridge, create unique impressions. Undoubtedly, some of the poem's expressive power is found among these strange image juxtapositions and the surprisingly strong emotions they evoke. García Lorca's poem is not a textbook, but an alarm clock, and a melting one at that.

Another example is Murakami Haruki's *Kafka on the Shore* (Murakami 2005). In the case of *Kafka on the Shore*, I have pondered it and struggled with its images but still do not understand even half of the surreal situations that Murakami depicts. In cases in which the text seems beyond the abilities of the translator to grasp, or when the things the translator does grasp — vague nuances, passing but disconnected images, seemingly unrelated happenings, apparently arbitrary idiosyncrasies of expression — do not properly compute, it may be time for the translator to give up on conscious analysis, let go of the steering wheel, and trust the author.

How does a translator "trust the author" in practical terms? By avoiding the extremes of over-interpretation (which may lead the text in an irrelevant direction) and elision of problematic material (which may eliminate something subtle but important). While the unreflective "triaging" of a text is often an insufficiently thorough approach, after reflection, the translator may in fact deem the text to be impervious to interpretative analysis. In such a situation, a relatively "literal" style of translation based on moment-to-moment noticing may turn out to be the best strategy, after all.

Understanding not only the things one notices, but why one notices those particular things, will be useful in helping translators avoid overlooking subtle but nevertheless important elements of a literary text. Knowing when real-time noticing is the best option available is a complementary skill that *still* depends upon being aware of the things that one is likely to miss.

7

NINE STATELY RAVENS

The expressive effect in Poe's blank verse [sic] poem "The Raven" lies in the repetitive rhyming of melancholy, disturbing words like "Nevermore," and "Lenore," words that blow in like a wind from some far-off, long-abandoned graveyard. Poe controls the overall motif of the poem by consciously repeating these words and thereby regularly reproducing the atmosphere that is expressed by each. If one were to take away such acoustic effects from "The Raven," nothing would remain except a meaningless row of letters. This being the case, is there any translator who could hope to successfully put the poem into Japanese? The futility of translating poetry should be apparent from viewing even a single line of such a translation.

Hagiwara Sakutarō

(1933: 92-93; Strack translation)

Judging from the epigraph, the poet Hagiwara Sakutarō seems to be of like mind with Shelley and Frost in his pessimism concerning the translation of poetry. Was the pessimism warranted? In this chapter I will take up Hagiwara's challenge and examine not one but nine Japanese translations of Edgar Allan Poe's "The Raven" to ascertain what exactly remains after the translator's difficult task is finished. Before proceeding, I will offer a few comments on the Japanese orthography that accompanies the excerpts.

Romanization of these excerpts follows *Kenkyusha's New Japanese English Dictionary*, 4th Edition (Masuda 1974). In some of the translations, older types of *hiragana* usage (*kana-zukai*) are evident. In such cases, orthography has been adapted to reflect the modern orthographic expression for corresponding sounds in modern speech, the rationale being that modern readers of the Japanese translations would tend to ignore the explicit older *kana-zukai* and instead internally vocalize the newer pronunciations. In cases where *kanji* and accompanying superscript readings do not coincide (a relatively common artifice called *ate-ji* in Japanese) or the superscript does not match standard orthography, Romanization follows that of the explicit superscript.

Translations 7.1 through 7.6 were originally published in vertical lines of type extending from the top to the bottom of the page with lines ordered across pages from right to left. While Translations 7.8 and 7.9 were in atypical formats which will be explained later, Translation 7.7 was originally published from left to right with lines ordered from top to bottom to better facilitate interlingual comparison with the original English poem. Lines of the translations originally published vertically have been realigned horizontally in this volume for the same reason.

The poems and translations included in this chapter are not complete. Due to space limitations, only the first 2 of 18 total stanzas of Poe's original poem "The Raven," have been excerpted. To compare complete versions of each translation with the original poem, please consult the translations in their originally published texts and formats. The excerpts of the Japanese translations of Poe's poem have been referenced using the name of each example's translator to clarify analysis.

Each translation excerpt includes the translated title of the poem in Japanese, the name of the translator (added here by the author of this volume to ensure that each translator is properly identified), and either one or two stanzas of the translation, these decisions being made based on analytical necessity. In the case of Translation 7.8, the author of this volume transcribed the spoken content from the work's audio track.

Poem 7.1

An Excerpt from "The Raven" (Poe 1845)

"The Raven"

by Edgar Allan Poe

Once upon a midnight dreary, while I pondered, weak and weary,

Over many a quaint and curious volume of forgotten lore —

While I nodded, nearly napping, suddenly there came a tapping,

As of some one gently rapping, rapping at my chamber door.

"'Tis some visitor," I muttered, "tapping at my chamber door —

Only this, and nothing more."

Ah, distinctly I remember it was in the bleak December;

And each separate dying ember wrought its ghost upon the floor.

Eagerly I wished the morrow; — vainly I had sought to borrow

From my books surcease of sorrow — sorrow for the lost Lenore —

For the rare and radiant maiden whom the angels name Lenore —

Nameless *here* for evermore.

Translation 7.1

An Excerpt from "*Ō-garasu*" (Saijō 1927)

「大鴉」

西條八十訳

一

わびしき夜更け、われ弱くくたびれごこち、

忘られし教の奇しき巻々に、

こころ潜めつ、いつとなく、うつらうつらと睡るとき、

にはかにかろく敲くおと、

誰びとか、いとひそやかに打つごとく、

わが室の扉をほとほとと、

「こは賓人」と呟きぬ、「わが室の扉をひたうつは」―

　　音のみ、かくて影はなし。

Ichi

Wabishiki yofuke, ware yowaku kutabire gokochi,

wasurareshi oshie no kushiki makimaki ni,

kokoro hisometsu, itsu to naku, utsura-utsura to neburu toki,

niwaka ni karoku tataku oto,

tarebito ka, ito hisoyaka ni utsu gotoku,

waga heya no to wo hoto-hoto to,

"ko wa marōdo" to tsubuyakinu, "waga heya no to wo hita'utsu wa"―

　　oto nomi, kakute kage wa nashi.

Translation 7.2

An Excerpt from "*Ō-garasu*" (Hinatsu 1935)

「大鴉」

日夏耿之介訳

むかし荒涼たる夜半なりけり　いたづき嬴れ黙坐しつも
忘郤の古学の蠹巻の奇古なるを繁に拔きて
黄妳のおろねぶりしつ交睫めば　忽然と叩叩の歔門あり。
この房室の扉をほとほとと　ひとありて剥啄の声あるごとく。
儂呟きぬ「賓客のこの房室の扉をほとほとと叩けるのみぞ。
　さは然のみ　あだごとならじ。」

Mukashi kōryō-taru yowa nari keri itazuki mitsure mokuza shitsu mo

bōkyaku no kogaku no fumi no kiko naru wo shiji ni hirakite

kōnei no oroneburi shitsu madoromeba kochinen to ton-ton no ogonai ari.

Kono heya no to wo hoto-hoto to hito arite hakutaku no koe aru gotoku.

Ware tsubuyakinu "marebito no kono heya no to wo hoto-hoto to tatakeru nomi zo.

Sa wa sa nomi adago to naraji."

Translation 7.3

An Excerpt from "*Ō-garasu*" (Abe 1967)

「大鴉」

阿部保訳

むかし凄涼の夜半のこと、私がやつれ疲れて、すでに人の忘れた学問の
おかしな珍奇な書物をあまた開いて、思いに耽っていたとき――
まるでうたたねでもするかのように、私が微睡んでいたとき、ほとほとと音が
聞えた。
誰かがそっと私の部屋の戸をこつこつと、叩いてでもいるかのように。
「誰だろう、」私は呟いた、「私の部屋の戸を叩いている――
　　　　それだけだ、何でもない。」

Mukashi seiryō no yowa no koto, watashi ga yatsure tsukarete, sude ni hito no wasureta gakumon no

okashi na chinki na shomotsu wo amata hiraite, omoi ni fuketteita toki―
maru de utatane de mo suru ka no yō ni, watashi ga madorondeita toki, hoto-hototo oto ga kikoeta.
Dare ka ga sotto watashi no heya no to wo kotsu-kotsu to, tataite de mo iru ka no yō ni.
"Dare darō," watashi wa tsubuyaita, "watashi no heya no to wo tataiteiru―
　　　　sore dake da, nan de mo nai."

Translation 7.4

An Excerpt from "*Karasu*" (Shimada 1969)

「鴉」

島田謹二訳

あるひと夜、荒涼たる真夜中のこと、力なく疲れ心地にうつらうつら、

忘られし学問のいにしえの奇<ruby>奇<rt>く</rt></ruby>しき<ruby>書<rt>ふみ</rt></ruby>の<ruby>上<rt>え</rt></ruby>、わが思い潜めいし時、——

うとうととまどろみかけつ、うなずきて眠りいし時、ほとほととにわかに軽く

叩く音。——

わが部屋のドアうち叩く、ほとほとと誰そやしずかに<ruby>敲<rt>たた</rt></ruby>く音。

われ呟きぬ——「こは<ruby>客人<rt>まろうど</rt></ruby>のわが部屋のドアをうつ音。

　　　　ただその音ぞ、その音のみぞ。」

*Aru hito yo, kōryōtaru mayonaka no koto, chikara naku tsukare gokochi ni utsura-
utsura,*

*wasurerareshi gakumon no inishie no kushiki fumi no e, waga omoi-hisomeishi
toki,*——

*uto-uto to madoromi kaketsu, unazukite nemuri ishi toki, hoto-hoto to niwaka ni
karuku tataku oto.*——

Waga heya no doa uchi tataku, hoto-hoto to ta soya shizuka ni tataku oto.

Ware tsubuyakinu ——*"Ko wa marōdo no waga heya no doa wo utsu oto.*

　　　Tada sono oto zo, sono oto nomi zo."

Translation 7.5

An Excerpt from "Ō-garasu" (Tanizaki 1970)

「大鴉」

谷崎精二訳

いともわびしき真夜中に
奇異なる数々の古書を閲し
物憂く、疲れ、まどろむ時、
やにわに響くほとほとと
わが部屋の戸をやさしく打つ音。
「部屋の戸打つは客なるか。
唯それだけの事にこそ。」とわれ眩きつ。

Ito mo wabishiki ma-yonaka ni

ki'i naru kazu-kazu no kosho wo kemishi

mono uku, tsukare, madoromu toki,

yaniwa ni hibiku hoto-hoto to

waga heya no to wo yasashiku utsu oto.

"Heya no to utsu wa kyaku naru ka.

Tada sore dake no koto ni koso." to ware tsubuyakitsu.

正しく思い出づるなれ、風吹きすさぶ師走
燃えさしの炉の薪、床に影を落し、
われ東雲を待ちわびて、レノアの亡き悲しみを
思い絶たんと書に向かえど詮なしや。
天使らがレノアと呼びし稀なる美女、
その名この世に消え失せぬ。

Masashiku omoi izuru nare, kaze fuki susabu shiwasu

moesashi no ro no takigi, toko ni kage wo otoshi,

ware shinonome wo machi-wabite, Renoa no naki kanashimi wo

omoi-tatan to fumi ni mukaedo sen nashi ya.

Tenshi-ra ga Renoa to yobishi mare naru bijo,

sono na kono yo ni kie-usenu.

Translation 7.6

An Excerpt from "*Karasu*" (Fukunaga 1970)

「鴉」

福永武彦訳

嘗てもの寂しい真夜中に、人の忘れた古い科学を書きしるした、
数々の珍しい書物の上に眼を通し、心も弱く疲れ果てて──
思わずもうとうととまどろみかけたその時に、ふと、こつこつと叩く音、
誰やらがそっとノックする音のよう、私の部屋の戸をひびかせて。
『ああ客か、』私は呟いた、『私の部屋の戸を叩くのは──
　　ただそれだけのこと、ほかにはない。』

Katsute mono-sabishii ma-yonaka ni, hito no wasureta furui kagaku wo kaki-shirushita,

kazu-kazu no mezurashii shomotsu no ue ni me wo tōshi, kokoro mo yowaku tsukare-hatete ──

omowazu mo uto-uto to madoromi kaketa sono toki ni, fu to, kotsu-kotsu to tataku oto,

dare yara ga sotto nokku suru oto no yō, watashi no heya no to wo hibikasete.

"Ā kyaku ka," watashi wa tsubuyaita, "watashi no heya no to wo tataku no wa ──

　　Tada sore dake no koto, hoka ni wa nai."

NINE STATELY RAVENS   *133*

Translation 7.7

An Excerpt from "*Ō-garasu*" (Kajima 1997)

「大鴉」

加島祥造訳

ある嵐もようの夜、それも陰気な真夜中のこと、
　　私はひとりぐったりとした気分で
もう忘れられた古い不思議な物語の数々を読んでいて――
思わずうとうとと睡りはじめた、と、とつぜん
　　こつ、こつ、こつ、という音
まるで誰かがこの部屋のドアを、
　　そっと叩くかのよう――
「誰かが訪ねてきて」と私はつぶやいた
　　「部屋のドアを叩いているのだ――
　　　　ただそれだけのこと、なんでもない」

Aru arashi moyō no yoru, sore mo inki na ma-yonaka no koto,
　　watashi wa hitori guttari to shita kibun de
mō wasurerareta furui fushigi na monogatari no kazu-kazu wo yondeite ―
omowazu uto-uto to nemuri-hajimeta, to, totsuzen
　　kotsu, kotsu, kotsu, to iu oto
maru de dare ka ga kono heya no doa wo,
　　sotto tataku ka no yō―
"dare ka ga tazunetekite" to watashi wa tsubuyaita
　　"heya no doa wo tataiteiru no da ―
　　　　tada sore dake no koto, nan de mo nai"

Translation 7.8

An Excerpt from "*Karasu*" (Simpsons: Japanese voice-over track 2005; Strack Transcription)

「鴉」

『ザ・シンプソンズ』吹き替え版の訳

物寂しい真夜中に

人の忘れた、珍しい書物の上に目を通し

心も弱く疲れ果て

まどろみかけた時に

こつこつと叩く音

誰やら　部屋の戸をそっとノックする音のよう

「ああ、客か」私は言った

私の部屋の戸を叩くのは

ただそれだけ他にはない

Mono-sabishii ma-yonaka ni

hito no wasureta, mezurashii shomotsu no ue ni me wo tōshi

kokoro mo yowaku tsukare-hate

madoromi-kaketa toki ni

kotsu-kotsu to tataku oto

dare yara heya no to wo sotto nokku suru oto no yō

"ā, kyaku ka" watashi wa itta

watashi no heya no to wo tataku no wa

tada sore dake hoka ni wa nai

Translation 7.9

An Excerpt from "*Karasu*" (Simpsons: Japanese subtitles 2005)

「カラス」

『ザ・シンプソンズ』字幕スーパー版

昔　荒涼たる夜半に

心も弱く疲れ果て

忘れ去られた珍しい書物に目を通し

まどろみかけた時

コツコツと叩く音

誰かが部屋の扉を叩く

客だなと私

誰かが私の部屋の扉を叩く

それだけのことだ

mukashi kōryō taru yowa ni

kokoro mo yowaku tsukare-hate

wasure-sarareta mezurashii shomotsu ni me wo tōshi

madoromi-kaketa toki

kotsu-kotsu to tataku oto

dare ka ga heya no tobira wo tataku

kyaku da na to watashi

dare ka ga watashi no heya no tobira wo tataku

sore dake no koto da

Experiment: "The Raven" Japanese Translation Assessment Survey

Through this book, I will assert that translations should be tied to specific goals so as to achieve the greatest possible equivalence in relationship to those goals. To demonstrate how translations will in fact vary according to the goals of the translator, I have chosen four apparently goal-oriented translations of Edgar Allan Poe's poem, "The Raven," and have administered a survey to determine if results corresponding to these purported goals are in fact evident in the translations. Statistical analysis will be used to corroborate my hypothesis. A description of the survey follows.

Method

The survey was administered to 136 students in a Japanese university. Students received class credit for participation. The results of 17 surveys were discarded because answers were incomplete and results from 3 surveys were discarded because respondents were not native Japanese speakers. Before assessing four Japanese translations of "The Raven" (Poe 1845), half of the students were given a 4-question survey designed to prime semantic attention and the other half were given a 7-question survey designed to prime auditory attention. It was thought that perhaps such priming questions might cause a significant level of disparity between the assessments of the respective groups.

Following the sets of priming questions, all participants proceeded to answer identical questions concerning two stanza excerpts from four translations of "The Raven." Participants viewed only four translations because it was thought that viewing any more than this number of translations would take too long, causing participants to lose concentration and thereby decreasing the quality of the survey's results. Specifically, the participants viewed excerpts from Translations 7.5, 7.6, 7.8, and 7.9 (the first stanza for each of these translations is included in this chapter). These particular translations were chosen after preliminary analysis because they did not include extensive archaicism (as translations 7.1 and 7.2 in particular do) and furthermore were judged to reflect the differing goals of their respective translators in translation.

The participants were asked to choose a single translated poem among the four that they felt best reflected the following subjective categories: "best overall quality" (最も優れている),"easiest to understand" (最も理解しやすい),"most poetic" (最も「詩的」),and "best-sounding" (最も響きのいい). "Best overall quality" was assessed first and participants did not know while assessing this category that three other more specific questions concerning the four translations would be asked. Participants were instructed not to change previous answers in light of subsequent responses. So as not to interfere with their judgments concerning these subjective aesthetic categories, the participants were not shown the original English poem and so had no basis for comparing translation "accuracy" (except for the possibility of making comparisons among the four translations themselves). In this sense, they were not making assessments of the quality of "translation" per se, but simply assessing the Japanese language results of the translation process.

Results

Results for the 116 native Japanese speakers who fully completed the survey are found in Table 7.1.

Table 7.1

"The Raven" Japanese Translations Assessment Survey Results

Category Assessed	Trans. 7.5	Trans. 7.6	Trans. 7.8	Trans. 7.9
Best Overall Quality	36 (31.0%)	29 (25%)	29 (25%)	22 (19%)
Easiest to Understand	0 (0.0%)	24 (20.7%)	59 (50.8%)	33 (28.5%)
Most Poetic	56 (48.3%)	23 (19.8%)	14 (12.1%)	23 (19.8%)
Best-sounding	71 (61.2%)	10 (8.6%)	16 (13.8%)	19 (16.4%)

With respect to the 4- and 7- question priming sets administered prior to analysis of the translations, there was no significant difference in assessments observed between the two groups for any of the categories.

As for results concerning the four categories mentioned in the method section, results were non-significant for the category "best overall quality" but significant for the rest of the categories. Specifically, results of participant judgments concerning "overall quality" among the four translations were non-significant, $x^2(3, N = 116) = 3.38$, p>.05. The number of participants that judged Translation 3 to be the "easiest to understand" was significant, $x^2(3, N = 116) = 61.45$, p<.01. The number of participants that did not judge Translation 1 to be the "easiest to understand" was also significant, $x^2(3, N = 116) = 61.45$, p<.01. The number of participants that judged Translation 1 to be the "most poetic" translation was significant, $x^2(3, N = 116) = 35.38$, p<.01. The number of participants that judged Translation 1 to be the "best-sounding" translation was significant, $x^2(3, N = 116) = 82.55$, p<.01.

Discussion

Concerning the 4- and 7-question sets that were intended to prime responses for either semantic or auditory effects, it was hypothesized that the priming would lead to a skewing of results between groups, with those primed for semantic effects and those primed for auditory effects tending to select different translations for the category "best overall quality." That such a significant outcome did not occur likely resulted from the fact that by the time participants had read through all four translations so as to assess them for "best overall quality" the effects of the earlier priming would have worn off. In retrospect, the semantic and auditory preliminary questions used in the priming aspect of the experiment were not well-matched with the content of the ensuing part of the test they were expected to prime.

The overall non-significant result for the category "best overall quality" was an unanticipated result. As the translations were very different, it was expected that the participants would naturally gravitate to one or another of the translations among the four. The fact that they did not is somewhat remarkable. If one were to examine different sets of translations, different results would likely be in evidence. Nevertheless, when translations with different representative features and of relatively good quality are evenly matched, participant opinions naturally fan out according to differences in personal preference.

Despite the fact that no single translation was judged to be better in terms of "best overall quality" than the others, when participants were asked to evaluate the four texts according to each of three different categories of literary value, each yielded statistically significant results in favor of a particular text and, for one category, against a particular text. Generally, these findings fall in line with the observations I have made about literary "qualities" in earlier chapters of this book. While the categories "easiest to understand," "most poetic," and "best-sounding" are all subjective categories, within a specified cultural group they are understood in more or less the same way. Furthermore, literary texts, when evaluated according to these culturally bound criteria, can yield statistically verifiable results with respect to those criteria.

To restate a previous analogy, while one can expect that different people will have different favorite colors, one would not expect people in the same cultural group to all have completely different opinions as to what constitutes the color "red." In this sense, literary works may be evaluated for specific culturally-motivated aesthetic qualities provided that the evaluation is done within that particular cultural group or subgroup.

Literary critic Stanley Fish has claimed that what fails to be mentioned by linguists in their analysis of literature is "precisely what constitutes literature" (Fish 1980: 98). In doing so, he mistakes reasonable attempts to verify the "qualities" of literature for impossible attempts to characterize the general "Quality" of literature. The "qualities" of literature, while varying from culture to culture, may nevertheless be intersubjectively verified. It is likely that such qualities can only be verified in a statistical manner, that is to say, linguists researching literature may never be able to produce broad, 100% perfect, no exceptions-type conclusions. Nevertheless, as we compare and contrast the varying results from different cultures, not only the possibilities of literature but the prevalent trends will become apparent.

Of course, within each tested cultural group or subgroup there are bound to be some who view literature differently from the mainstream. Due to the nature of radial categories, these opinions are valid but non-prototypical, statistical "outliers," beliefs that do not characterize the general thinking within the group. For this reason, in the scientific study of literature, the presence of dissenting opinions or examples that do not fit the general trends, rather than being seen as fatal flaws that threaten the legitimacy of the analysis in general, should be expected and regarded straightforwardly as noteworthy exceptions to the rule.

In the Methods section, I mentioned that the four translations examined by participants in the survey were chosen because they were thought to be representative examples of translations created with different goals for translation in mind. Specifically, Translations 7.5 (Tanizaki) and 7.6 (Fukunaga) were chosen for a combination of reasons. First of all, they are both relatively "authoritative" translations due to the fact that they have been included in two differing versions of Poe's collected works, both of these collections being published in 1970. The readership for these translations would likely include Poe scholars and other readers with a pre-existing interest in poetry and/or Poe.

Furthermore, while both translators are presumed to be Poe experts due to the inclusion of their translations in scholarly collections of Poe's works, they nevertheless display sharply differing strategies for translating the poem. Tanizaki's translation was one of the most compact among the nine and seemed to include the most noticeable auditory effects while Fukunaga's translation apparently eschewed concision while attempting to capture a maximum amount of the meaning and nuance of the original poem. Both of these authors were attempting to write a "literary" poem, but apparently with different ideals and therefore different goals as to which aspects they would emphasize: one highlighted auditory effects and the other stressed semantic aspects.

The two translations coming from the Japanese language version of a single episode of the animated television series, *The Simpsons*, were also presumed to have been designed with specific goals in mind. Translation 7.8 (Strack transcription) was created to be spoken by a narrator, accompanying the animated sequence developed to coincide with the English-language recitation of (excerpts from) Poe's original poem (Poe 1845: 94-100). For this reason, the translator or translators, no doubt working so as to meet a tight production deadline, were forced to make their translation as concise as possible so that it could be read aloud along with the animated sequence. They were further constrained to make the translation as easy to understand as possible so that its spoken rendition would be heard and understood not by literary scholars but by a general television viewing audience.

The other version from the same *The Simpsons* episode, Translation 7.9, is significantly different from the sound-track version and in fact represents an entirely new translation. This translation made for use in the episode's Japanese subtitles was created with the main constraint being that the maximum amount of information had to be packed into the smallest amount of screen space and fewest number of characters. Professional subtitle translator Yamasaki Kōtarō has noted that translators of subtitles in Japanese must ideally not exceed 4 characters per second of screen time (Yamasaki 2000: 143). The reason for this is that if this number of characters is exceeded, viewers cannot read them and still keep up with the action on the screen. Undoubtedly, the translator or translators of Translation 7.9 were translating with such constraints in mind as this unique translation was being composed.

In fact, did the varied goals of the translators result in translations that were different enough to effect results of the survey? The statistically verified answer is "yes." With respect to the category "easy to understand," the translation that garnered the most responses from participants who read all four translations to assess them was not one of the three translations designed to be "read" but the only translation designed to be "heard," namely Translation 7.8 (the transcription of the voice-over soundtrack from *The Simpsons*). In that this translation is relatively compact in form, does not include much difficult vocabulary, and reads very smoothly, it was natural that this translation would have been chosen by a significant number of participants with respect to this category.

A number of participants did select either Translation 7.6 (Fukunaga) or Translation 7.9 (*The Simpsons* subtitles) for this category. Nevertheless, the length of each line in Fukunaga's translation undoubtedly made it relatively more difficult to process. As for 7.9, a few marked and slightly archaic expressions (e.g. "*kōryō taru*") likely caused some respondents not to select it. No respondents at all selected Tanizaki's Translation 7.5 as the "easiest to understand." I would hypothesize that this occurred because Tanizaki, in his attempt to emphasize auditory effects, had to make compromises to do so. The effects achieved came at a certain relative semantic cost, as evident in the results for this particular category.

It should not be surprising then, that according to the survey results, Tanizaki's translation has indeed achieved some noticeable auditory effects. 61.2% of respondents selected Tanizaki's translation as being the "best-sounding" among the four while the other three translations split the remaining responses more or less evenly. There seems to be a difference in the conceptual categories "most poetic" and "best-sounding" in the minds of the Japanese participants. While Tanizaki's translation garnered 61.2% of responses for the category "best-sounding," he only received 48.3% of responses for the category "most poetic." It is clear that the Japanese concept of "poetry" includes a number of aspects, with auditory effects being but one aspect among these.

While Fukunaga's Translation 7.6 received a very low 12.1% of responses in the "best-sounding" category, it still managed to receive the second greatest number of responses in the category of "most poetic" behind Tanizaki. It would seem that Fukunaga's translation did not garner many responses because it did not fit the categories being tested for. Fukunaga's translation seems to have been the product of a desire to squeeze as much of the original meaning and nuance as possible into each line (resulting in very long lines). Unfortunately for this translation, participants were not asked to assess which translation best reflected the original meaning of Poe's English poem.

Auditory Aspects of "Poetic" Quality Viable in English to Japanese Translation

While no firm conclusions may be drawn and other strategies may indeed be possible, Tanizaki's translation (7.5) gives some clues as to an effective approach to reproducing English language auditory effects in Japanese translation. Figure 7.1 below shows the end and internal rhyming pattern for the first two stanzas of Poe's "The Raven." Each "=" sign represents a syllable. End rhyme that is consistent from stanza to stanza is indicated by rectangular enclosure (C). One slightly questionable case of internal rhyme has been indicated using an asterisk (*). Alliteration and assonance are also present in "The Raven" but have not been indicated in Figure 7.1.

Figure 7.2 shows the predominant vowel sound repetitions for the first two stanzas of Tanizaki's translation (7.5). Vowel sounds used three times or more in succession and repetitions of vowel sound combinations have been indicated by rectangular enclosure (I I). There are also multiple examples of vowel sounds being repeated only once evident in the translation but these effects are less noticeable and unnecessarily distract from the more prominent effects so, while they likely have auditory value as well, they have been omitted from Figure 7.2 below.

144

Figure 7.1

Pattern of End and Internal Rhyme in Stanzas 1 and 2 of Poem 7.1 (Poe)

= = = = = = AB = = = = = = AB

= = = = = = = A*B = = = = = = = $\boxed{C}$

= = = = = = DE = = = = = = DE

= = = = = = DEDE = = = = $\boxed{C}$

= = = = = = = = DE = = = = $\boxed{C}$

= = = = = = $\boxed{C}$

= = = = = = FG = = = = = = FG

= = = = = = FG = = = = = = $\boxed{C}$

= = = = = = HI = = = = = = HI

= = = = = = HIHI = = = = $\boxed{C}$

= = = = = = = = = = = = = = = $\boxed{C}$

= = = = = = $\boxed{C}$

Figure 7.2

Vowel Sound Repetitions in Stanzas 1 and 2 of Translation 7.5 (Tanizaki)

I O O A $\boxed{\text{I I I}}$ A O A A I

I I $\boxed{\text{A U A U A U}}$ $\boxed{\text{O O O O}}$ E I I

O O U U A E A O O U O I

A I A $\boxed{\text{I I I}}$ U $\boxed{\text{O O O O O}}$

A A E A $\boxed{\text{O O O}}$ A A I $\boxed{\text{U U U}}$ O O

E A O O U U A A $\boxed{\text{U A U A}}$

A A O E A E $\boxed{\text{O O O}}$ I $\boxed{\text{O O O}}$ A E U U A I U

A A I U O O I I U U $\boxed{\text{A E A E}}$ U I U A U I A U

O E A I $\boxed{\text{O O O}}$ A I I U A I A E $\boxed{\text{O O O}}$ I

A E I O O E O $\boxed{\text{A I A I}}$ E E $\boxed{\text{O A O A}}$ I A A I I O

O O I A A n O U I I U A E O A I A

E I A A E O A O O I I A E A U I O

O O A $\boxed{O\ O\ O}$ I $\boxed{E\ U\ E\ U}$

Although the first few lines of Tanizaki's Translation 7.5 do include a mild end rhyming on the vowel *i*, the effect quickly dissipates. Furthermore, although both the first and second stanzas end with the vowel *u*, this pattern does not continue uninterrupted through the third stanza (not included in the excerpt of Translation 7.5). Particularly with reference to end rhyme, Tanizaki begins with a brief attempt at recreating Poe's effect but does not sustain it, thereby failing to accomplish it at the level of consistency required to generate "unity of effect," an explicit goal which Poe in fact had hoped to achieve in the original English poem (Poe 1846: 157-159).

Tanizaki's poem does make use of other kinds of auditory repetition, however. The repetitions are both compact and abundant within stanzas and are exemplified by his use of phrases like "*kazu-kazu*" (meaning "many") in the second and "*hoto-hoto to*" (a light "rapping" sound) in the fourth line of the first stanza. Tanizaki also makes use of assonance by repeating vowel sounds, three or more times in some places. In this way, Tanizaki effectively recreates, if not the precise pattern of internal rhyme and assonance used by Poe, a frequency of use of similar effects that is sufficient for the reader to notice. This particular aspect of Tanizaki's poem, working mostly without reference to "rhythm" and "meter" in the English literature sense of the terms, is likely to contribute greatly to the fact that Tanizaki's poem was deemed to be the "best-sounding" of the four by a significant number of participants.

Tanizaki's *hoto-hoto* is an onomatopoeic expression. In that such onomatopoeic expressions in Japanese tend to rhyme internally within the expression itself (e.g. *pachi-pachi, kasa-kasa*; cf. chapter 4, this volume), seeing abundant use of such expressions is not surprising in that they appear to be the most efficient and unforced way to foreground auditory stimuli in the language. Indeed, in the first stanza alone, all 9 translations make use of onomatopoeic expressions in one form or another. In addition to *hoto-hoto* (used in translations 7.1, 7.2, 7.3, 7.4, and 7.5) and the equally popular *kotsu-kostu* (the sound of "knocking" on a door; used in 7.3, 7.6, 7.7, 7.8 and 7.9), we also notice *ton-ton* ("knock-knock"; 7.2), *utsura-utsura* (the sound of someone sleeping; 7.2 and 7.4), and *uto-uto* (also dozing; 7.4 and 7.6).

As has been mentioned before, because Japanese syllables (nearly) always end in one of the language's five pure vowel sounds, end rhyme is easy to achieve in Japanese but difficult to use as an attention-getting artifice. The fact that natural occurrences of such repetitions are profuse in the language ensures reader desensitization to all but the most exaggerated effects of this kind. Furthermore, because the pronunciation of Japanese written language is expressed by way of *hiragana*, a syllabary that does not explicitly separate vowels and consonants, alliteration (the repetition of consonant sounds without relation to accompanying vowels) tends to be less distinguishable, as well. For this reason, Tanizaki, in his attempt to mimic the kind of auditory effects found in "The Raven" has resorted to heavy use of assonance and internal rhyme to compensate for the other less viable options.

Tanizaki also achieves a sense of rhythm overall, but it pales in comparison to the original poem. The trochaic rhythm (with stress on the upbeat) and distinctive meter (octameter acataleptic; Poe 1846: 161) of Poe's poem combine to create an ever-increasing momentum to match the "phrenzied" (Poe 1846: 159) feelings of the protagonist as he hears "Nevermore" from the Raven in answer to one question after another. As the reader of the original English becomes accustomed to the rhyme scheme, she is likely to pick up speed, fairly flying to the poem's conclusion, in a state of nervous excitement. With respect to iconicity, the images depicted and general tone of the original poem have been well-matched with its auditory features.

By way of contrast, Japanese poetry is often read slowly and contemplatively, so as to fully appreciate each idea and the nuances found in each *kanji*. Japanese readers have been, perhaps, conditioned to read in this way through their frequent acquaintance with *tanka* and *haiku*, two relatively contemplative Japanese poetic forms. Tanizaki's translation does attempt to nudge the reader into a quicker tempo but lacking both the strong rhythm and end rhyme of the original it is a losing battle. Nevertheless, while the resulting effect produced by Tanizaki's translation is quite different from that of Poe, he has succeeded in highlighting the poem's "poetic" aspect in terms that native speakers of Japanese can readily appreciate. It would seem he has obeyed Rossetti's famous dictum characterizing the key issue in the translation of rhymed verse: "that a good poem shall not be turned into a bad one" (Rossetti 1992: 65).

Skill in translation lies in choosing the "right" word from among a number of options and, as Mark Twain has so aptly stated, "[t]he difference between the *almost right* word & the *right* word is really a large matter——'tis the difference between the lightning bug and the lightning" (Twain (1890) 1992: 946). Just as poets are sensitive to language, so are the translators of poetry. From the standpoint of the poetry translator working within a tradition, each small point of variation and newly discovered word or phrase signals translator identity and personal style. In a sense, straying too greatly from the translations of predecessors may even seem risky and somewhat rebellious. The completely original translator implicitly rejects the tradition.

To my knowledge, the earliest published translation of "The Raven" into Japanese (and there may be some even older versions extant that I have yet to locate) is Translation 7.1 by Saijō Yaso with Translation 7.2 by Hinatsu Kō nosuke following close after. Among the seven translations produced after this "first generation" of Raven translators, Tanizaki's translation in particular seems to be the most innovative. While possibly referencing a few previous translations in a limited fashion, he does not bow to convention but strains to compress both the meaning and auditory effects of the Poe poem into as few syllables as possible, thereby increasing the speed at which the reader can advance. It was undoubtedly an extremely difficult balancing act. Read by itself, the difficulty of what was attempted may not be clear, but the lengths to which Tanizaki went to forge a new type of "Raven" translation become evident through comparison with the other translations. His successes have revealed themselves to me through repeated reading, as happens with most good poetry.

Noticing Nuance in "The Raven"

The fact that Edgar Allan Poe's "The Raven" met with both critical and popular success is at least partly due to the way in which Poe has consistently blended such a cascade of foregrounded phonological artifice into one densely woven whole. To assume that the poem is simply a dizzying display of auditory effects, however, is to miss the point of those effects.

As has been noted earlier in this analysis, the end and internal rhyme, the meter, the alliteration, and the assonance all interact to give the poem its irresistible momentum. This combination of effects furthermore leads the reader into an agitation that matches the increasingly panicked psychological state of the narrator as the story progresses. In this sense, translators who strive to capture and condense as many auditory effects as possible (while still attempting to reflect the poem's general meaning), may unintentionally accomplish the same iconic relation to the narrative's semantic plane without even realizing that they are doing so.

Nevertheless, emphasizing one thing inevitably diminishes another. In this case, tradeoffs to accentuate the auditory often come at the expense of nuance, and sometimes metaphor. The ways in which subtle nuances can be affected may be illustrated by noting how each translator has dealt with the phrase "many a quaint and curious volume of forgotten lore" (Poe 1845: 94) in the poem's second line.

In Translation 7.1, Saijō uses the phrase "*wasurerareshi oshie no kushi-ki maki-maki*" (unusual scrolls of forgotten teachings). Generally, Saijō's poetic diction and his use of the word *kushiki* cause the phrase to seem rather archaic. His use of the word "*oshie*" (teachings) to express "lore" captures something of the word's sense with respect to oral traditions and folklore, that is, that "lore" can be something verbally passed on.

In Translation 7.2, Hinatsu phrases the line as the somewhat wordy "*bōkyaku no kogaku no fumi no kikonaru wo*" which might be retranslated back into English as "strange insect-eaten scrolls/books-of-old-learning consigned to oblivion." The *kanji* combination 蠹巻, fusing the Chinese character for the Japanese "*shimi*," indicating a destructive, paper-eating insect, with "*maki*," the character for a scroll (the form in which old documents were typically found at the time of Hinatsu's writing) is creative, compact and allusive but perhaps a bit overstated; the translation fails to communicate a sense that the book was "quaint" and rather conveys a sense that the book was likely "musty," a property not necessarily in keeping with the narrator's "richly furnished" surroundings (cf. Poe 1846: 162). It could be asserted, however, that while Poe had been attempting to portray loneliness in terms of "beauty" and "intense and pure elevation of soul" (Poe 1846: 154-155), the poem as a whole deals not with "loneliness" so much as "terror," and "beauty" not so much as "the uncanny." If one asserts this and assumes that Poe's intentions clearly did not match his results, then Hinatsu's translation of "quaint books" as "musty scrolls" accomplishes a unity of effect in the Japanese cultural context that Poe has missed in the original American context.

Abe's Translation 7.3 renders the phrase as "*sude ni hito no wasureta gakumon no okashi na chinki na shomotsu*" (amusing, curious, already forgotten-by-people academic book(s)), another rather wordy formulation. In "*chinki na*," Abe has found a first-rate option to correspond to the English word "curious." Abe's translation is the only one of the nine that uses this word. The others may not have used it because it is a rather uncommon word and thereby foregrounds itself in the stanza's context. His use of "*okashi na*" for "quaint," while also unique to his translation, is slightly less felicitous, as it connotes something interesting and possibly humorous but not necessarily out-of-fashion, as the word quaint subtly implies. Of course this sense is covered somewhat by the phrase "*hito ni wasureta*" so the loss is not total. In this case, the meaning of "lore" has expanded in the direction of scholarly books, possibly due to the influence of Hinatsu's "musty scroll" translation.

In Translation 7.4, Shimada echoes Saijō and Hinatsu with his phrase "*wasurerareshi gakumon no inishie no kushiki fumi*" (forgotten academic long-ago strange book(s)). Again the word choices emphasize the archaic rather than the sumptuous aspects of the poem's atmosphere.

In Translation 7.5, Tanizaki uses the compact phrase "*ki'i naru kazu-kazu no kosho*" (many strange old books), a phrase that retains the idea of "strange uniqueness" but peals away a bit of "magical" nuance from the word "lore." Undoubtedly in Tanizaki's translation, fine points of nuance have been foregone to enhance brevity and auditory aspects. The use of the sonically repetitive word "*kazu-kazu*" firmly indicates that the narrator is perusing more than a single book, as many of these translations neglect to indicate. The fact that the narrator's mind is wandering into stray thoughts is iconically paralleled by his unfocused reading. These meandering thought processes reflect the tendencies that cause him to produce the series of questions that will ultimately lead him to the brink of despair by the end of the poem.

Fukunaga's Translation 7.6 outdoes all of the others in terms of sheer verbosity. He translates the phrase as "*hito no wasureta furui kagaku wo kakishirushita, kazu-kazu no mezurashii shomotsu*" (many out-of-the-ordinary forgotten-by-people books [in which] old science is written). The use of the words "*furui kagaku*" seems to transform the word "lore" even further from the marginally acceptable "academic folklore" sense of the word into what seems to be almost an outdated science textbook, something that the narrator of Poe's poem would probably not have been reading.

Skipping over Translation 7.7 momentarily, the wording of Translation 7.8 (*The Simpsons* voice-over track) seems to be an abbreviated and essentialized version. It runs "*hito no wasureta, mezurashii shomotsu*" (forgotten-by-people out-of-the-ordinary books). This ruthless essentializing results in a relatively good and marketable product. Generally speaking, this voice-over track translation is admirable in the disciplined way it pares down the content of Poe's poem to produce an easily understood, somewhat schematic Japanese language replica of it. It is like those miniature models of the Eiffel Tower that are sold alongside the real thing in Paris. They lack crucial detail and pale beside the original, and yet the resemblance is unmistakable and they will fit in your suitcase. It is not surprising that this version was chosen as the "easiest to understand" of the four translations evaluated in the survey.

Translation 7.9 (*The Simpsons* sub-titles) uses the phrase "*wasure-sarareta mezurashii shomotsu*" (forgotten left-behind out-of-the-ordinary book(s)). While this version generally chooses from among the various standard options, the creative addition of *sarareta* (left-behind) adds a slight but felicitous item to the linguistic choices that future translators of "The Raven" will have at their disposal as they attempt to capture the nuances of this intricate poem. Reflecting on the fact that this translation was rated to be less "easy to understand" than 7.8, it seems likely that the decision to directly quote Hinatsu's archaic wording "*kōryō taru yowa*" makes this line in 7.9 more allusive and poetic than its counterpart in 7.8 but does this by introducing a potentially confusing phrase into the highly visible first stanza, thereby reducing the clarity of the stanza as a whole and the first line in particular.

Kajima's version (7.7) does the Poe translation tradition a great service by at long last noticing that the word "lore," at least in one of its senses, refers to "fantastic stories" or "legends." He translates the phrase "*mō wasurerareta furui fushigi na monogatari no kazu-kazu*" (many already forgotten old strange stories).

It should be noted that the influences of previous translations are not always a good thing. In the case of the word "lore," while Saijō's initial interpretation was relatively sound and Hinatsu's was well-matched to the Japanese cultural context of his day, extrapolations from these interpretations led in an unfortunate direction, away from the central idea of "legends and folk tales" and toward the less central nuance of "old science books." It almost seems as if, with respect to this one phrase, the translations of the first generation influenced subsequent translations even more than the particular words used by Poe in the poem itself. In this process, more or less accurate initial interpretations have been successively adapted and eventually transformed into mild mistranslation, mistranslation that is only detectable by going back to the original poem. This process continued until someone (in this case, Kajima) realized the conceptual drift away from Poe's original word choice and translated against the consensus of tradition to capture a more central sense of the (admittedly vague) word.

It would appear that certain instances of distinctive phrasing come to be, through sheer force of poetic sophistication, copied verbatim in some subsequent translations and used as stimuli for creative inspiration in others. Hinatsu's catchy and relatively accurate formulation "*kōryō taru yowa*" (荒涼たる夜半; bleak/desolate midnight) is found verbatim in two other translations and, in Abe's translation, has morphed into "*seiryō no yowa*" (凄涼の夜半; bleak/acutely-forlorn midnight) , an expression which says more than Poe's "midnight dreary" but does so eloquently and in a way that matches the overall tone of the poem. Hinatsu's use of the word "*madoromeba*" (to doze or nod off) seems to carry forward through "*madoronde*" to the throw-back diction of "*madoromi-kaketsu*", and finally reaches a thoroughly modern feeling of completion in "*madoromi-kaketa*" (slightly dozing/on the edge of dozing). This "*madoromu*" strain passes through all but two of the nine translations. Of course anyone with a good knowledge of English and Japanese or an interlingual dictionary could potentially arrive at some grammatical permutation of this particular "strain," so the presence of influence in specific cases cannot be confirmed with any certainty. Nevertheless, it seems that while precise influences may not be exactly pinpointed, translation of "The Raven" after the first generation has in some ways been a group task.

Concluding this discussion of the nuances of words in translation, one might say that, when translators like Tanizaki eliminate fine nuances in attempts to convey sonic aspects of the text in a compact way, some nuances are indeed lost but, if skillfully done, it is very possible for the core meaning to survive. In the reverse situation, however, when translations use more words in apparent attempts to squeeze every last drop of meaning from the source text, they often drift into errors and overstatements. I believe a lesson may be drawn from this. The key to capturing fine nuances in poetic translation does not lie in using more words, only better ones.

Can Metaphor in Poetry Survive Translation?

There are a couple of briefly mentioned metaphors that appear in the second line of Poe's second stanza (in this book, only excerpts for Poem 7.1 and Translation 7.5 include this second stanza). They are found in the phrase "each separate dying ember wrought its ghost upon the floor" of the original poem. It is difficult to pinpoint Poe's exact meaning in using this curious phrase. Six of the translations included here (specifically Translations 7.1, 7.2, 7.3, 7.4, 7.5, and 7.7) have interpreted this image to mean that the fire's embers, giving off their last light, cast shadows on the floor near the hearth. This may be a good translation of the material states, imagined by Poe, occurring in and near the depicted hearth. While what actually (at least in the story's context) happened with the embers in the fireplace is not expressed with utmost clarity, Poe's poetic metaphorical depiction of the situation seems more pertinent with respect to the poem as a whole.

The phrase, using the word "dying" to anthropomorphize the physical state of an ember that is burning out, is poetically extended to create a related metaphor using "ghost," representing the ember's indistinct state after "death." Perhaps Poe was picturing small glowing fragments of ash from the fireplace that fly into the air and subsequently burn out before hitting the floor, leaving only an indistinct dark smudge on the floor where they land. In any case, the two metaphors are explicitly correlated through the use of parallelism. Given the narrator's preoccupation with the death of his love, Lenore, such metaphors, when presented in parallel as they are, must be considered small factors that contribute to achieving an overall "unity of effect," the very ideal that Poe aspired to as he wrote the poem (Poe 1846: 158-159).

It is surprising, then, that only three of the translations (Translations 7.6, 7.8, and 7.9) have translated the word "ghost" as "*yūrei*" or "*rei*" (respectively meaning "ghost" and "spirit" in Japanese) and even more surprising that the anthropomorphized "death" of the ember does not survive the translation process in any of the nine cases. Fukunaga's Translation 7.6 is the first of the translations to explicitly translate the "ghost" aspect of this dual metaphor and, while his translation does a good job of developing the idea within the line, the parallelism that highlights it in the original text is lost.

In a sense, overlooking these metaphors does not represent a loss of haphazardly inserted poetic artifice but a loss of small but telling pieces of a larger puzzle, pieces that coalesce in the original to create strong resonance. While losing one of the two metaphors due to extenuating circumstances in translation is somewhat understandable, when six of nine translations lose *both* of the metaphors despite the fact that they had been foregrounded through parallelism, I can only conclude that, while implicitly understanding the metaphors, the translators deemed the (unclear) literal meaning of the line to be more important to translate than the (quite clear) metaphorical meaning. In other words, they took what Umberto Eco has called an "interpretive bet."

Eco notes that to decide how a text should be translated, translators need to make conjectures about the things that are pictured in the text and that "[o]nce the most reasonable conjecture has been made, the translators should make their linguistic decisions accordingly" (Eco 2003: 20). When ambiguous situations arise, translators will naturally make their decisions based on their previous conjectures. There is a risk involved in this. What if the translator's previous conjectures have been based on false premises?

In the case of the elision of the metaphors in stanza 2 of "The Raven," there seems to have been an assumption held by most of the translators that metaphors function only locally, carrying out a purely "ornamental" function in their specific location within the text. Indeed this is the case with some metaphors. But not in this case.

Admittedly, the exact reasons why each translator elided one or both of the metaphors are relatively unclear. Reader expectations for translations of poetry implicitly require that the translation mean the same thing as the original while simultaneously satisfying reader expectations for sensory pyrotechnics that exceed those found in everyday language. It is difficult to satisfy these conflicting sets of reader expectations at once. Given such a set of preconditions, when ambiguity is found in a very localized part of a literary text, especially ambiguity that can be cleared away easily through elision or linguistic circumvention, the translator faces a difficult choice: leave the ambiguity in place for the reader to struggle with or banish the ambiguity thereby creating a more "tidy" but less resonant translation.

It seems to me that this second strategy was utilized in the case of Poe's "dying" embers and "ghosts." Given the choice of providing the reader with a highly allusive but somewhat ambiguous metaphorical phrasing or a clear-cut literal interpretation that eliminates ambiguity, six of nine translators chose the latter option. Apparently they did not consider the fact that a "literalized" metaphor does not become less metaphorical but, in fact, entirely ceases to be a metaphor at all. This strategy, the "literalization of the figurative," results in a loss of allusive power, a power that may not be evident in a single line but nevertheless combines with other similar allusions as a part of a bigger metaphorical picture. In limited, specific cases, when metaphors are assumed to work locally and not globally, the results may be minimal but if metaphors are unreflectively culled throughout the translation of an entire literary work, the results may be semantically profound.

8

TRANSLATING AMBIGUITY

Your judgment of *Anna Karenina* seems wrong to me. On the contrary, I am proud of my architecture. But my vaults have been assembled in such a way that the keystone cannot be seen. Most of my effort has gone into that. The cohesion of the structure does not lie in the plot or in the relations (the meetings) of the characters, it is an internal cohesion...look well and you will find it.

Leo Tolstoy

(2000: xv)

Puns and other kinds of ambiguity are not in any way restricted to poetry but in fact are found often in the titles of short- and long-form narrative. Furthermore, these "puns" in many cases are not simply locally instantiated artifice for ornamental purposes, but clues put in place by the author precisely to lead the reader to broader metaphorical content diffused throughout the work. In this sense, they are difficult to translate not incidentally but precisely due to their function within the text: linking otherwise unconnected metaphorical domains to induce specific lines interpretation.

On Differing Viewpoints for Interpretation

In this chapter, I will assert that, in many cases, clues that allow the reader to match up metaphorical domains found in the text as a whole have been placed there purposefully by the author to encourage a particular interpretive viewpoint.

I am not asserting, however, that the "authorized" viewpoint as represented by these encoded clues is the only legitimate viewpoint, or even the best viewpoint, from which to interpret the text. From the standpoint of "organization," however, I take it for granted that a literary text will display, or at least make an effort to display, levels of organization and artifice not found in texts more generally. The cognitive category of "literature" carries such expectations (whether realistic or not) in tow. In this sense, one can analyze a literary work either with the goal of affirming the presence of such distinctive complexity, or with the opposite goal of deconstructing it and thereby denying that the complexity in it is in any way out of the ordinary. In either case, though, author encoded interpretive clues in certain literary works represent a desire on the part of such authors to achieve a "literary" level of sophistication.

Reasons for Reader Perception of Ambiguity

Before moving to specific examples of ambiguity found in the titles of literary works and then checking to see if this ambiguity has survived into the translations of these titles, I would like to clarify the vague term "ambiguity." I noted in chapter 6 that I do not have a good understanding of García Lorca's poem, "*Ciudad sin Sueño (Nocturno del Brooklyn Bridge)*" (García Lorca 1987: 95-96), even in its English translation, "Sleepless City (Brooklyn Bridge Nocturne)" (García Lorca 1990: 67-71). One explanation for my lack of comprehension is that the poem is written surrealistically and without explicitly logical construction, and therefore is, due to the intent of its author, resistant to analysis. Such poems and literature may need to be understood in a more intuitive way. Then again...maybe not. As I attempt to distinguish differing types of ambiguity in the following few paragraphs, I will do so by explaining a few more reasons why I might not be able to understand the poem.

1. Vagueness due to Reader Information Deficit

Perhaps the real reason that I don't understand García Lorca's poem lies in the fact that I have too little knowledge of Spanish or of New York or of García Lorca's other works, knowledge that other readers of García Lorca would likely have. With reference to Menard's translation of *Don Quijote de la Mancha*, Anthony Bonner has noted that "ambiguity is richness" (Steiner 1998: 74); this reference undoubtedly refers to the types of ambiguity I will mention later, but the term "richness" does not apply to the type of ambiguity (actually "vagueness"; cf. Tuggy 1993) I will explain now. Here, it is simply imprecise understanding due to lack of relevant information.

As I noted in chapter 3, for metaphor to be understood in literature, the reader must have a knowledge base built up for both conceptual domains. If either or both domains are not sufficiently filled out, then the metaphor will not be understood at the time, although it may be understood retrospectively once that knowledge has been acquired. Therefore, other people may already understand García Lorca's poem, but if I want to understand it, I may need to study some Spanish, or learn more about New York, or read a bit about García Lorca, or possibly all three. Experienced translators understand that there is no substitute for a firm grasp of background knowledge concerning whatever subjects happen to be depicted in a source text.

2. Encoded Ambiguity

"Encoded ambiguity" is the proper context in which to understand Bonner's comment about ambiguity being richness (Steiner 1998: 74). This view has been confirmed in experiments by Coulson, who concludes that "people not only tolerate ambiguity, they positively revel in it" (Coulson 2006: 257). Authors, in their desire to accentuate reader feelings of "interest" or perceptions of "depth" with respect to their text, often use ambiguity as a way to leverage associational activity.

As mentioned in chapter 3, "[s]tudies of the cross-modal priming task have produced evidence for momentary simultaneous activation of all senses of an ambiguous word, irrespective of relative frequency or contextual probability" (Cutler & Clifton 1999: 140). In this sense, polysemy (explained briefly in the following paragraph) offers authors the opportunity to stimulate a broader spectrum of the neural associational network than words with only a narrower range of meaning. If they can thereafter write the text in such a way as to include recurring details that further activate the conceptual domains of both of the meanings, when each detail is encountered they have increased the chance of creating reader interest and moved a step further toward the repeated activation necessary for entrenchment into long-term memory.

Croft and Cruse define the broad sense of polysemy as "variation in the construal of a word on different occasions" (Croft & Cruse 2004: 109). Each word has a meaning potential and with some words, such as "bank," the meaning construed will change according to the textual or real-world context in which it is perceived. Lakoff notes that polysemy is not just a matter of labeling things but is crucially tied to cognitive organization (Lakoff 1987: 333-334). As a related but somewhat different linguistic phenomenon, homonymy is the case in which two unrelated words sound the same but have different meanings. An example of homonymy would be the two unrelated words "pros" and "prose." In spoken English, the homonymy of these two words forms the basis for the pun in Example 8.1:

Example 8.1

"Amateur poets can improve their skills by studying the writing of pros/prose."

At first glance, one word may seem more salient than another but the actual meaning cannot be determined without specifying the context of the utterance

TRANSLATING AMBIGUITY   *161*

precisely. In Example 8.1, neither "pros" nor "prose" can be grammatically or semantically excluded from consideration without further grounds for construal. Examples of both homonymy and polysemy will be discussed in this chapter. Although the terms are not interchangeable, the effects they produce in literary context largely are.

So then, back to García Lorca. Supposing that I have enough background information to interpret his poem, yet I still notice some ambiguous words in it. It is very possible that I am dealing with purposefully instantiated polysemy or homophony. I will presume for the moment that authors do not use ambiguity to intentionally confuse the reader (as in Example 8.1 above), but to make two alternative interpretations of the poem equally viable, and thereby cause the poem to seem "richer" in Bonner's sense. Suppose that when García Lorca uses the word "*cielo*" in the first line, he is using it in such a way that it could mean either "sky" or "heaven." The meaning of the entire poem might change greatly depending on which meaning the reader uses as a basis for construal. In this case, the ambiguity in the original poem would indeed represent a form of richness in that it permits two possible interpretations. Consequently, the translator, instead of making an "interpretive bet," may rather choose the English language alternative that is more ambiguous (in this case, "heaven").

Of course such ambiguity may be instantiated in literary works in other ways, as well. Referring to drama, Booth gives an example of ambiguity instantiated through ambiguous characterization:

[A]ny unintentional ambiguities the playwright may leave in [the] play are to some extent removed by a good production; each director imposes [his or her] own interpretation by defining, with [the] innumerable devices of production, the potentially ambiguous elements. Though *Richard III* may be ambiguous in the sense of permitting both sympathetic and unsympathetic readings of King Richard, any particular production tends to follow one line or the other. But in the novel, every reader is his own producer. (Booth 1961: 387)

Perhaps this comment will highlight the potential problems for translators caused by ambiguity in a text; for translators, like directors of dramatic stage productions, have the practical ability to use various trade techniques to move the work away from ambiguity and toward thematic unity based on a single avenue of interpretation (specifically, their own).

While readers are free to interpret a work that is ambiguous in either of the two ways, or even in both ways from one reading to the next, translators are in a situation much more similar to the stage director. Generally, translators do not have the option of writing two versions of their translation. (To do so is not entirely out of the question, though, and might prove to be an interesting experiment.) Generally speaking, translators are forced either to decide between the two meanings of the polysemous word or else to find a way to express both potential meanings in another way. Such circumvention is often difficult. And all of this depends crucially on whether the translator notices the fact that "*cielo*" might mean either "sky" or "heaven." If the translator fails to notice, then the decision will be made by default, according to whichever type of construal of meaning the translator happens to perceive. As Thomas and Turner noted with regard to unconscious styles (Thomas & Turner 1994: 12), default choices may lead to outcomes that match the translator's goals or outcomes that do not but in either case the translator loses the ability to negotiate the choice.

In some cases, ambiguity may stem from grammatical indeterminacy, as I will explain with respect to the title of Nagai Kafū's short story, *Botan no kyaku* (Nagai 1909), later in this chapter. Ambiguity may also result when words or phrases are used that make it difficult to discover whether the statement was intended literally or metaphorically. For example, the phrase "the White House is falling apart" is potentially ambiguous because it could mean either that the people running the White House are disorganized and therefore the institution is not functioning properly or it could also mean that the physical building, the White House, is dilapidated. The context of such a statement will determine construal. In fact, many words we now see as having more than one meaning may have come to be polysemous as certain construals of creative metaphorical extension have calcified into dead metaphor. Such cases exemplify Ralph Waldo Emerson's observation that "Language is fossil poetry" (Emerson 1844: 73).

So far I have been characterizing ambiguity as an either/or, binary Gestalt-type effect that is in a way analogous to the well-documented visual tendency which ensures a person "never see[s] a mixture of the two versions [of an ambiguous image presented]—it's always one coherent whole" (Feldman 2006: 6). With respect to polysemy, when an ambiguous word or phrase is understood by way of one of its contexts it will lead to a certain construal and when an ambiguous word is understood by way of an alternative context it will lead to a different construal. In some cases, though, there may be three or more differing potential construals resulting from the word or phrase's polysemy. In such cases, even identifying the source of ambiguity as polysemy may be difficult to achieve and the reader may be left without an explicit realization of ambiguity but only with a vague sense of resonance or depth.

With this in mind, I'm once again not sure how to interpret García Lorca's poem. After developing my cognitive bases for interpretation and reading it multiple times, I sense that there is something else there, something more complex than simply the binary difference between interpretations that construe "*cielo*" as sky or heaven, respectively. What kind of ambiguity is this?

There are two ways to interpret such a deep sense of ambiguity. It could be that we have hit a wall and must return to our starting position, namely that the poem, because of the way in which it was written, is resistant to interpretation and analysis. On the other hand, it is also possible that the ambiguity being experienced by the reader is a "holographic" type of ambiguity due not to the impossibility of analysis but to the complexity of the problem that needs to be analyzed. Perhaps there are multiple viewpoints from which construals can be formed. This situation will result not in a flip-flopping Gestalt-type pairing of interpretations, but a series of differing interpretations that exceed one another in their semantic relevance as each in turn is provisionally tested as a basis for interpretation.

Perhaps García Lorca's poem has been put together as a sort of semiotic puzzle in which the "bridge," the "sky," and the "iguanas" that "bite the men who don't dream" (García Lorca 1990: 67) all mean different things from different points of view. If this is the case, the text is not incoherent, merely prohibitively difficult to decode.

On the Correlation of Ambiguous Titles with the Presence of Diffused-domain Metaphor

Polysemy (or homophony) and metaphor often work in tandem in literary texts, with polysemous titles often providing important clues that leverage the reader's attention and thereby evoke specific lines of interpretation. It should be stressed, however, that not all authors necessarily use such a strategy and not all works necessarily display such characteristics.

On Puns and *Kakekotoba*

In the English language tradition, the word "pun" typically brings to mind the relatively unfunny verbal gags of a failing stand-up comic. In short, puns in the English language cultural context have an image problem: they are generally thought to be unsophisticated. Interestingly, the very same artifice seems more sophisticated when referred to as "double-entendre," a term originating in French. In the Japanese literary tradition puns can be facetious but do not necessarily imply a "laugh-out-loud" humorous sense. While Japanese does have a word for the bad-joke variety of pun (*dajare*), Japanese literature provides an alternative expression, the term *kakekotoba* (掛詞). *Kakekotoba* means a word or phrase from which two different meanings "hang," thereby resulting in unresolved ambiguity between the meanings. In all likelihood, *kakekotoba* has been a useful aesthetic idea for nearly as long as Japanese literature has been written.

Of course, English has a more sophisticated word for the idea as well, except that only linguists tend to know of it. With reference to poetry and not to titles of literary works, Roman Jakobson used the term "paronomasia"; he reflected that "[t]he pun [. . .] reigns over poetic art, and whether its rule is absolute or limited, poetry by definition is untranslatable" (Jakobson 1959: 434). Of course, the truth of this statement depends entirely on the definition of "translatable." Jakobson's opinion with specific reference to paranomasia echoes Shelley's general opinion quoted in the preface of this book.

It should be noted that translators do at times encounter a "lucky break" or two with regard to such puns. For example, one common *kakekotoba* in Japanese involves the strategic use of the *hiragana* combination *matsu* to simultaneously denote "waiting" and "pine tree" (cf. Shinmura 1991: 461). Because the use of Chinese characters will effectively disambiguate this homophony, *kanji* typically go unused and the word is simply written in *hiragana*. Translators of Japanese poetry into English were quick to notice that the English word "pine" (a tree) and the verb "to pine" (longingly wait for or think of someone) together result in homophony that is somewhat analogous to the Japanese *kakekotoba*, "*matsu*." In that *matsu* in Japanese means "to wait" generally and "pining" usually implies the narrow context of longing (and waiting) for someone to return affection, the match is not exact. Nevertheless, it is a lucky correspondence.

Such chance correspondences aside, though, is translating polysemous words into another language generally out of the question? In the following section, I will note some cases in which puns have been successfully translated into another language and also demonstrate the way in which strategically instantiated *kakekotoba* are placed in titles precisely to provide links between conceptual domains of metaphor diffused throughout literary works.

Noticing *Kakekotoba* in the Titles of Literary Works

While many literary scholars have noted in passing the "puns" evident in the titles of individual literary works, they have generally failed to recognize the great extent to which this strategy has been applied. Perhaps this has occurred because literary scholars, often limiting the scope of their study to a single author, assume such use of paronomasia to be a local effect, idiosyncratic to the particular author they happen to be researching. Furthermore, paronomasia, especially in the case of long-form narrative works is difficult to detect because often an understanding of the literary work as a whole is a prerequisite condition for the recognition of the polysemy or homophony of a word or phrase in that work's title.

Using nine relatively well-known works from the English-language and Japanese-language literary traditions, the remainder of this chapter will demonstrate three things: first, how these works include polysemy or other types of ambiguity in their titles, and secondly, how such ambiguity does not represent random artifice but has been specifically designed to match up metaphorical domains in the respective narratives. Finally, the examples will be used to show that, counter to the assertions of Jakobson and others, ambiguity has been successfully retained in the titles of multiple Japanese-language or English-language translations.

Heart of Darkness and *Oku no hosomichi*

In Robert Conrad's novel, *Heart of Darkness* (Conrad 1902), the character Marlowe travels by boat along an African river and as he does so he experiences spiritual darkness and moral degeneracy that culminate in his meeting with Kurtz. The journey into the "heart" of Africa is seen to debase and corrupt all who take it, the veneer of civilization diminishing as people travel further from civilized society. While comprising an ultimately anti-imperialist message, Conrad's *Heart of Darkness* nevertheless metaphorically expresses this message according to imperialist logic, emphasizing as it does the supposedly "irrational" aspects of uncivilized "dark" societies.

In fact, the title of the story, *Heart of Darkness*, contains polysemy that reflects this double movement in the story, namely the uncivilized "darkness" that Marlowe experiences as he travels into the Congo, the "heart" of Africa, and the increasing "darkness" that manifests itself in the "heart" (essential character) of those who proceed down the river. With respect to the story's paired metaphorical domains, JOURNEY TO UNCIVILIZED AREA and MORAL DEVOLUTION, we find not one but two types of polysemy functioning in the title. The word "heart" refers both to the centrality of the area in Africa to be visited and the essential character of its inhabitants, while the word "darkness" simultaneously indicates the purportedly "uncivilized" nature of the central African area and the essential nature of Kurtz's character after his moral acclimation to his surroundings. Explicit analyses of these metaphorical domains exposes the chauvinistic logic of Conrad's conceptualization of the story.

Faced with not one but two polysemous words in the title of Conrad's work, what are the chances that a Japanese translator would be able to, contrary to Jakobson's assertion, capture them both in the title of the Japanese translation? Not bad, as it turns out. The title for Conrad's story in Japanese, *Yami no oku* (『闇の奥』; Conrad 1958), uses the word *yami* to access the same polysemy evident in the English word "darkness." Because the conceptualization of "darkness" in Japanese can be understood both in terms of "immorality" on the individual human level and as a quality associated with an "uncivilized" area on the societal level, the polysemy carries across to Japanese without noticeable loss of grounds for ambivalent construal.

The translation of the word "heart" in Conrad's title is somewhat less straightforward. Undoubtedly, the translator considered using the Japanese word for "heart," *kokoro* (心) in the translated title. Unfortunately, while the word *kokoro* easily connotes essential human character and does indeed carry with it a limited sense of centrality, the idea of "centrality" in Japanese is usually communicated using a more common, related term, "*chūshin*," (中心). Although both words contain the Chinese character for "heart," they are not polysemous due to the fact that one *kanji* is read according to its *kun-yomi* (Japanese pronunciation) and one is read using its *on-yomi* (Chinese pronunciation). In contrast to the word "darkness," straight polysemy seems not to be possible with respect to the word "heart."

The translator, instead, has located an extremely allusive alternative. In place of the English "heart" he uses *oku* (奥), a *kanji* indicating both the "deep interior" of an area or "essential nature" of an idea or values system. In some ways, this particular option was somewhat predictable. The use of the term *oku* to simultaneously represent a "central, inland area" and "the essential nature of an idea" exactly parallels the title of *haiku* poet Matsu Bashō's early 18th century poetic travel memoir *Oku no hosomichi* (『奥の細道』; Matsuo 1702). Bashō's work describes an actual journey he took to the *michin'oku* (陸奥, or "inland") area (already mentioned in Poem 5.1 of chapter 5) in the Hokuriku and Tōhoku regions of northern Japan. In that the trip has been characterized as the journey of a wandering poet in search of essential aesthetic values in a relatively inaccessible rural area of Japan, the theme of spiritual enlightenment accompanying physical movement along the journey's path is foregrounded. Bashō's difficult spiritual pilgrimage to higher ideals represents a movement that is inverted yet ultimately similar to Kurtz's descent into spiritual depravity in Conrad's novel, and so the highly allusive title that the translator, Nakano, has chosen for *Heart of Darkness* not only captures the polysemy but even thrives in its Japanese literary context.

This being the case, one might expect that the inverse would be true as well. That is, if the polysemy in the title *Heart of Darkness* can be successfully translated into Japanese, then the polysemy evident in Bashō's *Oku no hosomichi* 『奥の細道』 (Matsuo 1702) should survive translation into English in a similar way. In fact, results have been mixed. There have been a number of prominent published translations of the title into English, some of these including Britton's *Narrow Road to a Far Province* (Matsuo 1974), Yuasa's *The Narrow Road to the Deep North* (Matsuo 1966), and Keene's *The Narrow Road to Oku* (Matsuo 1996).

Britton's English title captures the least of the original title's polysemy of the three. Emphasizing the great distance that must be traveled, use of the expression "Far Province" emphasizes the exotic aspects of Bashō's journey rather than the "essentialness" of the aesthetics he was attempting to discover. Such a title makes Bashō seem like little more than a tourist. While the title may have other redeeming qualities that recommend it, if the criterion for judgment is defined by the use of polysemy in the title to prefigure the metaphorical orientation of Bashō's work as a whole, the title is a failure.

Yuasa's translation is better at retaining the original's polysemy. He renders the Japanese word *oku* as "Deep North," simultaneously capturing the relative direction from Edo of the area visited and, somewhat imprecisely, the "depth" of the aesthetic ideas Bashō was attempting to uncover there. There is a slight nuance problem, however. In the European literary tradition, the term "North" has strong "Nordic" and Wagnerian associations (cf. Carpenter 1997: 5). Because such an atmosphere is entirely dissonant with the type of aesthetic Bashō was attempting to seek out, the phrase "Deep North" is less than ideal when subtle nuances are considered.

It may be useful to elaborate on why a translator will be unlikely to use "heart" to express *oku* in English just as Nakano has used *oku* to so successfully express "heart" in Japanese. In carrying out such a strategy, one word that comes to mind is the term, "heartland." Unfortunately, this term, at least for

Americans, brings to mind images of vast plains of wheat and pickup trucks. Another possibility would be to express the title as *Narrow Road to the Heart of (Haiku/Japan/x)*. The problem here stems from the fact that the original title does not specify exactly what Bashō was seeking on his journey and so such a translation will unnecessarily disambiguate Bashō's title, which, like his *haiku*, thrives on indirection. Omitting the final word and its tendency to overspecify meaning, one could translate it obliquely as *Narrow Road to the Heart*. The problem here is that the "heart" in English tends to express emotional or sentimental centrality more than aesthetic centrality.

Keene uses a different strategy. Rather than translating the difficult term *Oku* he transliterates it and adds commentary (Matsuo 1996: 9, 11) to explain to the reader the word's deep connotations with reference to Bashō's journey. This strategy has the advantage of retention of subtle nuance but the disadvantage of loss of "immediacy" in that it may take some time for the new meaning to register in the reader's conceptual system. Definitions, while very useful in a limited sense, are no substitute for conceptual categories. A native speaker's conceptual categories are fully integrated with multiple modalities of sense perception and carry the potential for immediate emotional response. In contrast to the potential resonance that preexisting conceptual categories have for the reader who reads the poem in the original language, newly minted definitions appended to transliterated foreign terms lack any type of entrenched associations at all and are therefore uncompelling for the reader of the poem in translation.

In this sense, the strategy of transliteration (translation that relies on pedantic, dry definition rather than immediately resonant conceptual association), may succeed in activating both domains of the polysemous title but is likely to do so in an overspecified manner that explains rather than presents the ambiguity. The reader's chance to experience metaphor in the work spontaneously is more or less precluded. In movie review terminology, transliteration accompanied by commentary represents a "spoiler"; that is, commentary that reveals key details of the story and may spoil the moviegoer's ability to spontaneously experience the movie. Nevertheless, it must be admitted that transliteration of the original word at least technically retains the word's polysemy, making it a relatively good compromise strategy when no other better options are available.

"Babylon Revisited"

"Babylon Revisited" (1931) is F. Scott Fitzgerald's story of Charles J. Wales (Charlie) and his quest to once again become the legal guardian of his daughter, Honoria, a few years after his wife Helen's death, a death that his sister-in-law Marion has blamed on his negligence. Charlie goes to visit Marion to convince her that he is no longer living the life of dissipation he had been living while his wife was alive. Unfortunately, some former friends from his wild Paris days find out where he is and follow him to the house. There they make a scene and embarrass Charlie, ruining his chances of being reunited with Honoria.

In the story, Fitzgerald uses Charlie's crossings of the "logical Seine" (Fitzgerald 1931: 617) to emphasize the discontinuity between the Right Bank and the Left Bank of Paris, and to portray Charlie's past in terms of the two. The story begins in a bar at the Ritz Hotel on the Right Bank (cf. Fitch 1989: 156), thus invoking his heavy drinking before Helen's death. He then proceeds by taxi to the Left Bank with its "provincialism" (Fitzgerald 1931: 618). During this transition, Charlie admits to himself that, while living in Paris, he had "spoiled the city" for himself, implying that he wished he would have spent more time with his family. This is confirmed by the fact that Honoria's place of current residence, located on the "provincial" Left Bank, turns out to be a place where his change of heart is not acknowledged. The twist of fate that wrecks Charlie's aspirations at the conclusion of the story shows that while he has attempted to leave his "Right Bank" Paris associations in the past, the past can never be completely left behind.

The story's metaphorical title, "Babylon Revisited," is ambiguous in two respects. The word "revisited" usually implies "going to a previously visited place again" but in some cases implies simply "recalling past experiences." Because Charlie has just arrived back in Paris after working for a time in Prague, the reader at first assumes the title to be referring to the fact that he is "revisiting" Paris, likened to Babylon. Exactly why Paris should be referred to as Babylon is not made explicit, although readers are probably assumed to know that the ancient city of Babylon is characterized in the Bible as a city of great corruption and cruelty (e.g. Psalm 137). Apparently the reader's already formed conceptualization of Paris will be required to intuit any corresponding elements between the two domains of this metaphor.

As the plot progresses, however, and the terrible results of Charlie's previous life of dissipation become clear, "Babylon" is seen to refer not to Paris generally but to a particularly dissolute time period in Charlie's life. The title, "Babylon Revisited," then, represents the use of polysemy for the purpose of temporary misdirection. At first, as the title seems to refer to Charlie's return to Paris, it will be slightly perplexing but in retrospect, once Charlie's personal history is understood, the title's meaning becomes clear. In this case, it might be said that the first construal of the title is not refuted, merely displaced by a more compelling construal once the reader can understand it in light of the story's overall plot.

There have been a number of translations of the title of "Babylon Revisited" into Japanese, including Shimizu's "*Ame no asa pari ni shisu*" (「雨の朝巴里に死す」; Fitzgerald 1955), Saeki's "*Babiron saihō*" (「バビロン再訪」; Fitzgerald 1957b, 1992b) , and Murakami's "*Babiron ni kaeru*" (「バビロンに帰る」; Fitzgerald 1999). The first translated title incorporates neither the idea of "Babylon" nor "Revisited." This title literally means "rainy morning, dying in Paris." While evocative and stylistically reminiscent of many highly dramatic titles in Japanese literary tradition, this title is mostly unrelated to the original Fitzgerald story. The name was chosen so as to capitalize on the release of the 1954 motion picture, *The Last Time I Saw Paris* (Brooks 1954). Because the plot of the movie was very loosely based on the story "Babylon Revisited," the Japanese title of the motion picture was simply appended to the translation without reference to the fact that no one dies in the rain in Fitzgerald's short story. In terms of ambiguity, this title does not retain any but creates it afresh, or at least confusion. Clearly in this case, equivalency was not assessed in terms of semantics but in terms of yen.

Saeki's and Murakami's titles are similar, both transliterating Babylon directly from English and thereby referencing whatever knowledge of the English concept of "Babylon" Japanese readers might have. As Japanese readers would be only somewhat less likely to realize the negative implications of a reference to Babylon than their English-speaking counterparts, this strategy represents a very pragmatic compromise. In fact, although not in common usage, the word *babiron* may be regarded as a foreign loan word not without conceptual associations in the Japanese language context.

With respect to the difference between "*saihō*" (再訪) and "*kaeru*" (帰る), however, the first is well-capable of indicating either a "return to an already visited place" or "reminiscence on previous events" but the second primarily indicates only "return to an already visited place." In that the initial misdirection in Fitzgerald's title involves "return to a place" which is finally supplanted by the idea of "reminiscence" and the agonized "reliving" of an unhappy previous stage in charlie's life, Saeki's translation using "*saihō*" retains the polysemy of the original while Murakami's "*kaeru*," centering as it does on physical return, diminishes it.

"May Day"

"May Day" (Fitzgerald 1920), already mentioned in chapter 6, is a complicated story involving many characters but the plot may generally be characterized in terms of chaos in New York City as many kinds of people, rich and poor, the

174

well-placed and the unemployed, former soldiers and communist newspaper workers, interact. The title "May Day" explicitly refers to events that take place on May 1st, Labor Day, a day with special significance for communists. The title is polysemous in that it is a homophone for "mayday," a distress signal used in the context of two-way radio communication. As with "Babylon Revisited," the second "distress-signal" aspect of the homophony, an apparent reference to the "distressing" state of social relations in New York at the time, will only be understood in retrospect if it is noticed at all.

The Japanese title of the translation, even in a number of different versions by different translators, has almost invariably been published as *Mei dei* (「メイ・デイ」; Fitzgerald 1992a). It departs from the normal Japanese transliteration of the May 1st holiday, Labor Day, in that the holiday is expressed as "*mēdē*." The title then, avoids explicit reference to the holiday and rather juxtaposes transliterations of the words "May" and "Day" as distinct lexical entities. The reason for artificially linking the two words in this way undoubtedly lies in the fact that a "mayday" signal in Japan can be expressed either by way of the Japanese expression *sōnanshingō* (遭難信号) or using the foreign loan expression *es-ō-es* (エス-オー-エス; S-O-S). The compromise option *Mei dei* represents an attempt to retain polysemy through segmented transliteration after other more straightforward options were examined and rejected.

A Farewell to Arms

A Farewell to Arms (Hemingway 1929; cf. Strack 2006b) recounts the war-time experiences of Frederic Henry, an American serving as lieutenant and ambulance driver for the Italian army in the first World War. In Book I, Frederic meets nurse Catherine Barkley, is soon wounded at the front and is thereafter sent to Milan to get his severely injured knee repaired. Book II recounts details of the couple's romance after Catherine is transferred to his hospital in Milan to care for him.

TRANSLATING AMBIGUITY   *175*

Just as he leaves Milan to return to the front, Frederic learns that Catherine is pregnant.

Book III begins with Frederic Henry's return to the front just before it is overrun by enemy soldiers. Underestimating the speed of the enemy advance, Frederic is unable to move the ambulances in his charge into friendly territory, getting them bogged down in back roads and fields during the retreat. Making his way on foot and dodging enemy patrols, one of his subordinates is killed and another deserts but eventually Frederic does reach the Tagliamento River and apparent safety. While crossing the bridge, however, Lieutenant Henry is arrested and thereafter discovers that Italian officers are being summarily executed by their compatriots for roles they are assumed to have played in the defeat. Seizing the opportunity when the attention of his captors is focused elsewhere, Frederic escapes into the river and is carried downstream. Emerging from the river, he begins to travel towards Milan.

Book IV tells of Frederic and Catherine's flight from the Italian authorities and escape to Switzerland by boat across a lake in the middle of the night in the rain. Book V recounts their time together in Switzerland. They are arrested soon after arriving but explain themselves well enough to be allowed to stay. Living in hotels and chalets, they spend a happy time together waiting for the birth of their child. Finally, however, Catherine and the baby both die after protracted labor.

The title of *A Farewell to Arms* (Hemingway 1929) is homophonous because the word "arms" may be understood to indicate either "weapons" or "human embrace." Because Lieutenant Henry deserts during the retreat in Book III, the reader will naturally assume after that point that the title refers solely to his desertion. When Frederic's new wife Catherine dies in childbirth at the end of Book V, however, suddenly a new meaning may be construed. The old meaning of desertion is retained but suddenly the story as a whole may also be seen in terms of events leading inexorably toward Frederic's loss of Catherine.

In the story's context, exactly what the relationship is between the war and Catherine's death is not clear. The homophony of the title presents the two construals "side-by-side" as well. That is, both seem equally salient in terms of the story's plot. Nevertheless, the construal of "arms" as weapons is by far the more natural of the two meanings in a decontextualized reading of the title. In fact, it is entirely possible that many (or even the majority of) readers, never consciously notice the homophony at all and simply assume that the title refers solely to Frederic's desertion.

The Japanese translation, while failing to reference the homophony evident in English, nevertheless implies that the novel is more than simply the story of Frederic's desertion. By phrasing the Japanese title *Buki yo saraba* (『武器よさらば』; Hemingway 1951) meaning "If weapons were to depart" or "If there were no weapons," the translator Ōkubo subtly implies two things. First, he indicates that the events of the story occur because Frederic decided to leave his weapons behind. This is the more explicit way to construe the title. Secondly, however, there is an implication that perhaps if the war had not occurred in the first place, Catherine would not have died.

In that Ōkubo was translating this story in 1951, just after the end of Japan's horrific experience in World War II, it is not surprising that a Japanese translator would create a title that tends to link the tragic ending of the story to the tragic nature of war itself. While perhaps implying slightly more than Hemingway's original title did, *Buki yo saraba* is both poetic and memorable. And in the final analysis, despite the failure to retain homophony, it does allude to another possible interpretation in the story. Ambiguity has been retained using a strategy often used in Japanese communication generally: high-context use of somewhat vague but nevertheless potentially communicative allusion.

"An Occurrence at Owl Creek Bridge"

"An Occurrence at Owl Creek Bridge" (Bierce 1890) begins with a depiction of a man about to be hanged from a railroad bridge during the US Civil War. Peyton Farquhar is a southern plantation owner who is tricked into attempting to destroy a strategically important railroad bridge. In fact the bridge is well-guarded, as Farquhar discovers when he is captured and sentenced to be hanged from the bridge. As he awaits his execution, he closes his eyes. When the plank he stands on is released and Farquhar falls from the bridge with the noose around his neck, he experiences a series of perceptions that leads him to believe that the rope has broken and he is miraculously falling towards the river below.

Enduring intense pain from the noose while bobbing and spinning along in the river's current, he eventually emerges from the river and makes his way home to his family, some thirty miles distant. In fact, however, as the story ends, his dead body is depicted as hanging from the bridge. His imagined escape had simply been the result of fragmented momentary perceptions being misinterpreted by his keenly focused but irretrievably traumatized subjective experience.

Before reading the story, the reader will likely assume that the "occurrence" at Owl Creek Bridge refers to some unusual incident that will happen as Farquhar is being hanged, but the end of the story reveals this construal to have been a semantic dead end. Nothing out of the ordinary, no "occurrence" has happened, except inside the mind of the hanged man, now dead. Unless one reinterprets the word "occurrence" to mean something that "occurred to Farquhar," that is, something he suddenly thought of as he was about to be hanged from Owl Creek Bridge, it is difficult to reconcile the title of the work with the story. In fact, Bierce has made subtle use of diffused-domain metaphor instantiated into the details of depiction to further confuse the reader and add interest to the story (Strack 2006b: 6-7).

Do the Japanese titles offer any kind of polysemy that allow for reinterpretation of the initial "dead-end" construal evident in the English title? The titles identified to carry out this study are relatively similar to one another. They are "*Auru kurīkubashi no ichi jiken*" (「アウル・クリーク橋の一事件」; Bierce 1969) which means "a single happening/incident at Owl Creek Bridge" and "*Auru kurīku tekkyō de no dekigoto*" (「アウル・クリーク鉄橋での出来事」; Bierce 2000) which means "an event at Owl Creek Iron Bridge." Both of these titles translate "occurrence" straightforwardly in terms of an unusual event and thereby reflect only the initial "dead-end" construal of the English title, neither title evoking an alternative sense to displace the first in retrospect. In that readers of the original work as well may potentially miss the well-concealed polysemy present in this title, even in retrospect, perhaps it would have been surprising had the polysemy in either of the translations been retained.

"The Bridge-Builders"

In "The Bridge-Builders" (Kipling 1898), a British engineer named Findlayson is overseeing the construction of a new bridge across the Ganges River. From the outset of the story, the river is referred to as "Mother Gunga" and Peroo, the Indian foreman, believes that because the construction goes against the will of the local Indian gods, the bridge is bound to be destroyed by the river. In fact, as the plot unfolds, a storm upriver sends a flood that threatens to wash the bridge away just before its completion. At this point Peroo offers Findlayson some opium to calm his nerves. Under the influence of the opium the two bridge-builders fall into an unsecured boat and are swept away by the flood.

Downstream they come aground on an island where they witness "a supernatural council of the local gods, each taking the form of an animal. Coming before the council as a crocodile, Mother Gunga attempts to persuade the others to destroy the bridge, her own efforts having been unsuccessful. Some gods agree with her that the bridge-builders have indeed gone too far" (Strack 2006a: 39) but others argue that the efforts of the "bridge-builders" will come to nothing. In the end, Findlayson and Peroo are rescued from the island and they return to find the bridge intact.

In a paper that detailed how Kipling painstakingly instantiates the metaphorical domains of this story, I noted how the term "bridge-builders" when used by the local deities, does not in fact refer to Findlayson and Peroo but actually refers to "empire-builders" (Strack 2006a). In this sense, the key metaphor in the story is EMPIRE-BUILDERS ARE BRIDGE-BUILDERS. The interdomain link that connects these two domains is found in a speech by one of the deities that describes the "bridge-builders" as coming from across the water and bringing with them their "fire-carriage," that is, their railway locomotive (Kipling 1898: 31). Because the interdomain link centers on a metaphorical interpretation of the term "bridge-builders," the title "The Bridge-Builders" is seen not only as a literal reference to the engineers but a metaphorical reference to empire-builders generally.

While there is a very good word available in Japanese for bridge-builders, *kyōryōka* (橋梁家), unfortunately this word overspecifies the fact that the bridge-builders in question are engineers actually constructing a physical bridge. Because the English word "bridge-builder" in Kipling's title is not a specialist's term but a general reference, it is more easily used for metaphorical purposes. For this reason, the translator of the Japanese text, Hashimoto, uses a slightly marked but more general substitute term in his title, "*Hashi wo tsukuru mono tachi*" (「橋を造る者たち」; Kipling 1995). This title literally means "people/individuals [who] build bridge(s)". The word *mono* in this usage does not overspecify the fact that the "individuals" referred to are bridge construction engineers by occupation. As such Hashimoto has created a sufficiently polysemous title that can refer to Findlayson and Peroo as the narrative opens and then enlarge itself as the story proceeds to include imperialists generally by the story's end.

180

"*Botan no kyaku*"

"*Botan no kyaku*" (「牡丹の客」; Nagai 1909) by Nagai Kafū represents an example that uses not polysemy or homophony but grammatical ambiguity to reference one literal and one metaphorical interpretation. In this short story (already mentioned in previous chapters), the narrator and a geisha named Koren travel by boat along a river and a canal in Tokyo to view the famous peonies of Honjō on a whim. As they travel, there are discussions of their future together. The geisha suggests that marriage might be a possibility but the narrator responds that they would just become tired of it in the end and then what? Finally arriving at the peonies, they discover the fabled flowers to be past peak, dingy, and ragged. Disappointed, they begin the trip back to the starting point of the excursion.

In the title, *Botan no kyaku,* the word *botan* is a word that can indicate peony flowers in either singular or plural and *no* is a possessive that links *botan* to *kyaku,* which generally means "guest" or "customer," but in this case seems closer to the English word "fare" in the sense that a taxi driver might "pick up fares." Judging from everyday usage and also the fact that the customers are paying passengers on a boat, *Botan no kyaku* would normally be construed as "the customers on their way to see the peonies" (from the boat operator's perspective). Nevertheless, the title is grammatically polysemous. In terms of potential construal without regard to context, the grammar of the title could be understood to indicate that the "customers (themselves) are peonies." Of course, such a construal, without any sort of context to provide grounds for it, would be nonsensical. As if to get the better of common sense, Nagai provides just such a context for construal when the narrator views the sorry shape of the flowers:

> Most of the peonies, however, had already begun to lose their petals. Even
> the flowers remaining intact had so lost their ardent coloring that the pistils
> stood out large and black. The blossoms, which would have properly scat-

TRANSLATING AMBIGUITY   *181*

tered long before if only they had been exposed to strong sunlight and brac-
ing wind, had been artificially induced to maintain their bloom; deep fatigue
and boredom seemed to emanate from each flower, flowing toward us and
blending in perfectly with our own feelings. (Nagai 1909: 72; Strack translation)

As the narrator explicitly compares the feelings of the couple with the state of
the flowers toward the end of the story, we find that the author has created a polysemous title that will only be understood as polysemy in retrospect.

Again, the question is, will the translator notice the polysemy and take
advantage of it to accentuate the story's metaphorical domains or not? In
Seidensticker's translation, "The Peony Garden" (Nagai 1972; briefly quoted in
Chapter 3 of this volume), the inter-domain link is not retained. By emphasizing the "garden" aspect of the trip, neither the reference to the main characters
on their trip nor to the explicit link between the state of the flowers and the state
of the couple's relationship as explicitly mentioned by the narrator are referred
to. Of course, the metaphor is retained through references in the text itself.
Nevertheless, without polysemy in the title to hint at this metaphor and emphasize it through repetition, the reader is unlikely to notice it or consider it important.

There are a number of possible titles that could have been used to retain
the ambiguity (and thereby maintain the efficacy of the interdomain link) in the
title. The obvious possibility, the direct translation of *Botan no kyaku* to "The
Peony Customers" admittedly sounds a bit unusual in English. The phrase
implies that the customers would be buying some peonies, which the two in
Nagai's story most decidedly do not do. The title "The Peony Passengers" as well,
does not work. It sounds like the two would be riding down the river on a peony.
Nevertheless, there are a few realistic possibilities that would retain grammatical ambiguity similar to that found in the original title, including "The Peony

182

Viewers" and "The Peony Excursion."

The Great Gatsby

The central figure in F. Scott Fitzgerald's novel, *The Great Gatsby* (Fitzgerald 1925), is Jay Gatsby, a man of considerable charisma who suddenly appears in the New York City vicinity and uses his money to gain friends by throwing lavish parties at his palatial home. With hopes of impressing and winning over a woman he had fallen in love with years earlier, now married to another man, Gatsby gradually arranges events and situations so that for a time it even seems that the two might end up together. Finally, however, an unforeseen tragedy occurs and his plans are brought to nothing.

By the end of the story, readers will understand the English title *The Great Gatsby* to have an element of irony about it; Gatsby turns out not to be so "Great" after all. The question I have is this: if Fitzgerald simply intended to briefly instill in the readers a sense of Gatsby as a figure of historical importance along the lines of "Napoleon the Great" or "Alexander the Great" so that it would seem ironic in retrospect, why didn't he give the story the title "Gatsby the Great"?

This is what the translator of one of the first versions of the story in Japanese has done by titling it *Idai naru gyattsubī* (『偉大なるギャッツビー』; Fitzgerald 1957b) . The specific formulation "*idai naru*" has generally been used in association with figures of military or political importance. Jay Gatsby does not seem to fit such an image. Another Japanese translation reflects Gatsby's style: lavish and gaudy. The straightforward title *Karei naru gyattsubī* (『華麗 なるギャッツビー』; Fitzgerald 1957a) may be literally retranslated back into English as "The magnificent/gorgeous Gatsby." While "The Gorgeous Gatsby" has a quirky alliterative ring to it, this type of title as well does not seem to capture perfectly what the author was trying to express. And furthermore, if, from the context of the story, a case could be made for using a word meaning "gor-

geous" in the title, an equally compelling case could be made for Gatsby's por-
trayal as a "great" guy, in the everyday sense of someone who is "likable." After
all, Gatsby was nothing if not likable, at least as depicted by the openly sympathetic narrator.

A further possibility presents itself. In the pre-Great Depression vaudeville era of America, magicians were extremely popular. These illusionists often
went by names like "The Great Blackstone" ("Harry Blackstone, Sr."), or "The
Great Leon" ("The Great Leon"). By the nature of polysemy, construal of meaning must be matched against context. Is there anything in the story's context that
would allow the reader to interpret Jay Gatsby as a magician? While the story
does occur during this same vaudeville era, no explicit references to magicians
are in evidence. There is however, one representative scene, referred to a second time by the narrator at the story's end, in which Gatsby holds out his arms
"toward the dark water in a curious way"and concentrates on the green light he
saw shining at the end of Daisy's dock (Fitzgerald 1925: 27-28, 158). While
Gatsby's gesture vaguely mirrors the theatrics of a magician during a performance, the gesture itself is, in the end, ambiguous.

The fact that one ambiguous sense of the polysemous phrase *The Great
Gatsby* implies Jay Gatsby to be an "illusionist" is all the more telling in light
of the story's overall plot. According to the narrative, to win Daisy, first Gatsby
transforms himself from a normal person to the center of gravity of the New York
social scene. Then he attempts to transform not only himself but those around
him so that he can attain his dreams. The construal of Gatsby as illusionist is a
perfect fit for the story.

Do any of the Japanese titles for the novel allow for this construal? Only
one. Murakami has resorted to transliteration and used the title "*Gurēto
gyattsubī*" (『グレート・ギャッツビー』; Fitzgerald 2006). In this case, due to
the fact that *gurēto* is a foreign loan word in Japanese and because potential construals for the highly polysemous word "great" in English are so abundant,

transliteration would seem to be the best option available.

Concerning the Retention of Ambiguity in the Translation of Titles

Works with polysemous, homophonous or otherwise ambiguous titles mentioned in detail in the preceding discussion have been compiled to form Table 8.1, including judgments concerning whether the ambiguity in the translated versions of the titles listed have retained ambiguity or not. In cases in which transliteration of the source language has resulted in the retention of overall ambiguity in the target text, an asterisk (*) has been added to each "yes"-answer to indicate the fact. The results of analysis of ambiguous titles in translation (see Table 8.1) demonstrate two things. First of all, these results show that many types of ambiguity (including polysemy, homophony, and grammatical ambiguity) are indeed potentially translatable. Judging from the results achieved by Japanese to English and English to Japanese translators of the literary works mentioned in this chapter, there is no reason to state categorically that paronomasia precludes translatability (Jakobson 1959: 434). In exactly half of the cases analyzed, translators identified solutions that allowed them to retain ambiguity in the target-language title. Furthermore, translators have crafted translations that can not only parallel the original ambiguous nature of these so-called "puns," but even match them in terms of role they play in the text, namely acting as interdomain links connecting relatively inconspicuous alternative interpretations for each respective work.

The second observation that may be drawn from the examples listed in Table 8.1 is that there are a number of relatively predictable factors that will affect whether the translation of polysemous words or phrases (or other types of ambiguity) can be accomplished or not. These factors include the following:

TRANSLATING AMBIGUITY   *185*

Table 8.1

Literary Works with Ambiguity Evident in the Title

Title	Ambiguity Type	Translated Title(s)	Ambiguity Retained?
Heart of Darkness	polysemy	『闇の奥』	yes
		(Yami no oku)	
『奥の細道』	polysemy	*Narrow Road to a Far Province*	no
(Oku no hosomichi)			
		The Narrow Road to the Deep North	yes
		The Narrow Road to Oku	yes*
"Babylon Revisited"	polysemy	「雨の朝巴里に死す」	no
		(Ame no asa pari ni shisu)	
		「バビロン再訪」	yes
		(Babiron saihō)	
		「バビロンに帰る」	no
		(Babiron ni kaeru)	
"May Day"	homophony	「メイ・デイ」	yes*
		(Mei dei)	
A Farewell to Arms	homophony	『武器よさらば』	yes
		(Buki yo saraba)	
"An Occurrence at Owl Creek Bridge"	polysemy	「アウル・クリーク橋の一事件」	no
		(Auru kurīkubashi no ichi jiken)	
		「アウル・クリーク鉄橋での出来事」	no
		(Auru kurīku tekkyō de no dekigoto)	
"The Bridge-Builders"	polysemy	「橋を造る者たち」	yes
		(Hashi wo tsukuru mono tachi)	
「牡丹の客」	grammatical ambiguity	"The Peony Garden"	no
(Botan no kyaku)			
The Great Gatsby	polysemy	『偉大なるギャッツビー』	no
		(Idai naru Gyattsubī)	
		『華麗なるギャッツビー』	no
		(Karei naru Gyattsubī)	
		『グレート・ギャッツビー』	yes*
		(Gurēto Gyattsubī)	

1. **Whether the translator notes the presence of the ambiguity.**

(For example, it seems likely that both Japanese translators of "An Occurrence at Owl Creek Bridge" overlooked the polysemy in the title.)

2. **Whether the ambiguous words or concepts in the source language are commensurable with words or concepts in the target language.**

(For example, the issue of whether the complex conceptualization of the English word "heart" in *Heart of Darkness* that implies both "centrality" and "essentiality" would find a single Japanese parallel that could simultaneously imply the same ideas.)

3. **Whether commensurable words or concepts that are similarly ambiguous include unwanted extraneous aspects that might prove a distraction.**

(For example, the unwanted culture-specific nuances that would accompany the word "heartland" as a relatively commensurable option when translating the Japanese word *oku*.)

4. **Whether the ambiguity can be accomplished by some means other than polysemy or homophony.**

(For example, the way that the translator of *A Farewell to Arms* used a grammatically incomplete and therefore semantically underspecified title to hint that there might be an alternative interpretation to the story in its Japanese title *Buki yo saraba*.)

5. **Whether transliteration is a reasonable option when other good options are not available.**

(For example, the way that transliterating the English word "Great" in *The Great Gatsby* seemed to be the only way to retain the broad range of potential construals associated with the highly polysemous English word "great.")

There is another important variable, as well: the determination of a translator to find solutions to problems that initially appear intractable. To the extent that translators believe that the translation of *kakekotoba*-type effects is impossible, they will not make the attempt. Furthermore, to the extent that they are unaware of the potential importance of such phenomena as interdomain links that can cue metaphorical understanding, they will be tempted to compromise quickly and move on.

Aside from the relevance of this chapter to translation, I hope that the previous examples have sufficiently demonstrated the way in which interdomain links of diffused-domain metaphors function surreptitiously in the titles of works in which those domains are instantiated, and also the fact that this phenomenon may be much more widespread than has been previously acknowledged.

9

SURVIVAL

National literature does not mean much these days; now is the age of world
literature, and every one must contribute to hasten the arrival of that age.

Johann Wolfgang Von Goethe

(1827)

The history of the modern novel is an example of interlingual and intercultural
accommodation, as Moretti has detailed (Moretti 1999). Not surprisingly,
translation played a prominent role in this process. With respect to Japan,
Futabatei Shimei (1864-1909) was one of the pioneers of the modern Japanese
novel. Before going on to publish *Ukigumo* (1887) (The Drifting Cloud), considered to be the first novel written in colloquial Japanese, he produced a translation of Turgenev's novel, *Fathers and Sons* (1862), remarkable for its unprece-
dented narrative style.

According to Keene (1984: 109), although Futabatei implied in his translator's introduction that he had created an entirely new narrative manner, in fact
he had perhaps imitated the speech stylings of celebrated raconteur (in Japanese,
落語家) San'yūtei Enchō (at the suggestion of his mentor, the famed critic and
translator, Tsubouchi Shōyō). The actual extent of the pioneer author's stylistic
originality aside, Futabatei's refusal to translate *Fathers and Sons* according to
the less colloquial orthodox style current in Japan at the time led more or less
directly to his later success as a novelist. Futabatei's decision not to bow to convention as a translator eventually contributed to the success of the novel as a

Japanese literary form.

It has been asserted that as globalization continues, translation is getting easier. Famed French literature translator Horiguchi Daigaku (1892-1981) put it this way:

> It was 40 years ago, when our country had not yet experienced westerniza-
> tion of lifestyle to the extent we have today. At present, one can translate the
> statement "he buttered his toast and ate it" without a second thought, but
> then, one would have had to say "he spread congealed cow-milk fat onto his
> roasted dough lump and ate it." At the time there were no words like "toast"
> or "butter" which could be used directly. (Horiguchi 1958: 9; Strack trans-
> lation)

As Japanese eat more tortilla chips and Americans eat more sushi, the wall of cultural difference which caused countless headaches for the translators of Horiguchi's generation seems to have been breached at certain points.

Murakami Haruki, Intercultural Accomodation, and Translation

It should not be any surprise that literary authors have noticed these areas in which the walls of intercultural "non-compatibility" are crumbling and have taken advantage of them. Jay Rubin, English translator of Japanese novelist Murakami Haruki, has noticed something similar about Murakami's literature: in the original Japanese, the stories have a certain "buttery flavor" (Rubin), but-ter being a typically "Western" taste in contrast to soy sauce or *miso* bean paste. Rubin notes, however, that once translated into English, this "buttery flavor" dis-appears completely, leaving only the story itself.

What accounts for this "buttery flavor" in Murakami's Japanese prose? There may be a number of factors, but among the most obvious are the choices of cultural artifacts Murakami chooses to depict. The best example may be the unpretentious ways the author makes reference to the Beatles song "Norwegian Wood (This Bird Has Flown)" (Lennon & McCartney 1965) in his novel, *Norwegian Wood* (Murakami 1991). Another factor is that Murakami, whose prolific record as a translator of American literature perfectly complements his considerable output as an author both in volume and in quality, includes ample references to various foreign works in his novels. Characters in "Norwegian Wood" explicitly make multiple references to Thomas Mann's *Magic Mountain* (Murakami 1991: 193) and F. Scott Fitzgerald's *The Great Gatsby* (Murakami 1991: 208), which Murakami went on to translate (Fitzgerald 2006).

Another noteworthy aspect is Murakami's choice of titles; almost inevitably, his titles translate perfectly into English. From *Kafka on the Shore* (2005) to *The Wind-up Bird Chronicle* (1997), Murakami's sense of what makes a good title seems to include "translatability into English" as an overt selection criterion. The title of his work, *South of the Border, West of the Sun* (1999), which contains an obvious riddle-like reference to Japan (the name of the country in Japanese, *Nihon*, means "origin of the sun"), also includes the somewhat marked phrase *Kokkyō no minami* (literally, "border" "of" "south") in its Japanese original. It would take an extremely obstinate translator not to follow Murakami's lead by phrasing the first half of this title *South of the Border*, an expression that has an appealing ring for Americans in particular.

Given Murakami's extensive experience as a translator, one even begins to wonder which is the translation of which. While the Japanese title may be more conceptually compelling due to the symbolic allusiveness of the sun in Japanese culture, the title's English translation exemplifies Murakami's "perfect pitch" (with respect to Western culture) which, at least to some extent, accounts for his great following among European and North American readers.

Increasingly, writers have begun to define success not in national but in international terms. To the extent that it is possible to do so, writers who can write in one language with a keen understanding of the stresses of the translation process (and can predict which aspects of their works will survive that process) are writing with a great advantage. Works that are extensively bound to a single language and culture may never break free from that culture's orbit. Conversely, it could be asserted that works that do break free will have done so precisely because of the recurrent literary values that are found in them. Goethe's prediction (quoted as this chapter's epigraph) concerning the ever-increasing emergence of an overarching *Weltliteratur* (Goethe 1827) seems more true with each passing year.

It is a sad and disturbing trend when viewed from the perspective of cultures that are losing out. House perceives this in terms of an ever-quickening pace of cultural "filtering" (House 2002: 107) accompanied by a "bland cultural universalism" (House 2002: 108) as Anglophone cultural norms are hybridized with other cultures. It may be said that the days of viewing the literary author as a small-scale artisan working only with the tools and materials offered by that author's immediate cultural and linguistic environment are soon to pass, if not long gone already.

Simultaneously, as globalization proceeds, translation becomes somewhat easier, not only because of trends toward intercultural accommodation but also because new generations of translators increasingly have access to insights even from beyond the borders of their own translation tradition. Such insights may allow them to, incrementally, move closer to that practically unattainable vanishing-point known as "equivalence."

Approaching Equivalence

The notion of "equivalence" has been a long-standing chimera in the study of literary translation. Tabakowska notes that the idea has been "rejected either as merely a special case of a more comprehensive (but equally vague) notion of functional adequacy" or alternatively understood "as an unattainable goal" or in terms of "similarity of response" or "explicitly acknowledged and then understood in many different ways" (Tabakowska 1993: 2). Reflecting on how the results of translation tend to follow from the goals of the individual translator, I wonder if having multiple types of equivalency is less of a problem than a solution.

Various subfields of translation have had relatively more success in detailing practical standards by which equivalence can be judged. The equivalence of an interlingual pair of diplomatic documents, ostensibly "twinned" through intense negotiations between official representatives of the nations involved, may be judged equivalent if the two countries are able to both accept and adapt to the words agreed upon in those documents (Kitamura 2000: 137). Such a standard of equivalence is extremely pragmatic. It seems to say that if no one notices any problems with the documents then there are no problems.

In the booming Japanese business translation industry, "equivalence" only becomes an issue in cases when the translator obviously strays from industry standards for "target language fluency" and "accuracy." In such cases, the translator may never even be told of the perceived problems, the primary repercussion being that they will not be contracted to translate again. In the "real world," equivalence is not theoretical but is, in fact, a "real issue."

In the case of literature, however, due to the complexity of the text needing translation, the standard to be used for evaluating equivalence has never been obvious. How is it that literary translation has even taken place in a context in which no two translators can completely agree on which aspects of a text must be expressed to achieve "equivalence"? While positive answers to this question inevitably revolve around personal value judgments of the individual translator, negative answers to the question may be more forthcoming. While equivalence as a positive value can only be characterized by the translator herself, factors that negatively influence equivalence may affect all translators equally. In part to review some of the issues brought up in this volume, I will attempt to characterize a few such factors.

Factors that Negatively Affect Equivalence in Literary Translation

One factor that negatively affects equivalence in literary translation is **The Assumption that the Author is not Strategically Using Hidden Artifice**. Although there may be some authors that in fact do not make strategic use of hidden artifice in their stories, to simply assume that authors do not carefully craft their stories is reckless, especially in light of the evidence available. The quotation from Tolstoy about the hidden architecture in *Anna Karenina* at the beginning of chapter 8 attests to this fact. To mention another example, during an interview, when Ernest Hemingway was asked about how the titles of his works were arrived at, he replied: "I would make a list of titles *after* I've finished the story or the book — sometimes as many as 100. Then I start eliminating them, sometimes all of them" (Reynolds 1976: 65-66). Such a calculating strategy for choosing titles belies the popular reputation Hemingway enjoyed. With respect to the author's reputation as a "natural" writer, Hemingway scholar Michael Reynolds notes:

> It is amusing to read through the early reviews, not for their appreciation of
> [*A Farewell to Arms*], but for the misconception of Hemingway-as-writer
> that were already current. He was anti-intellectual; he had learned too much
> from Gertrude Stein; he was an autobiographic writer; he wrote well natu-
> rally, but did not understand the process; he was unread; the image was full
> blown by 1930, and, if it was not true, it did not hurt his sales. (Reynolds
> 1976: 82)

In this sense, readers who assume that Hemingway does not strategically use literary artifice in his stories will be Hemingway's ideal readers. They can enjoy the effects produced by the hidden artifice without even suspecting that they are being cognitively manipulated. As for translation however, a translator who makes the same assumption about Hemingway will also be an ideal reader, but she will not be an ideal translator. Such a translator is likely to translate the "moment-to-moment experiences" of reading while missing the effects that are not foregrounded in perception. Translators that allow more prominent effects to completely eclipse less prominent ones risk damaging aspects of a literary work's equivalence that they did not even realize were present.

In making the previous observation, I am not suggesting that works that seem to be indeterminate in some way should be over-interpreted. The history of literary criticism includes many examples of attempts to banish ambiguity from texts that do not offer a comfortable sense of completion. Of particular note is Popova's chapter (Popova 2002) in *Cognitive Stylistics: Language and Cognition in Text Analysis* (Semino & Culpepper 2002) which characterizes how various scholars have attempted to "solve" the ambiguity "problem" in Henry James's story *The Figure in the Carpet* (James 1964). With reference to a specific passage from Milton, Fish makes a similar point with reference to critical interpretations. He correctly observes that "[w]hat is not available is the connecting word or sustained syntactical unit which would pressure us to decide between [ambiguous senses], and in the absence of that pressure, we are not obliged to decide" (Fish 1980: 117). The act of eliding or disambiguating ambiguity found in a text not only presupposes that a "tidy transparent translation" (Snel Trampus 2002: 38) is automatically a better one but, more problematically, also assumes that the author didn't really know what she was doing.

A Translator's Ideological Outlook and Social Viewpoint can at times negatively affect equivalence. Koster has noted recent trends in post-structuralism which tend to evaluate translations in terms of "ideological, social and cultural implications" (Koster 2002: 24). For example, there are a number of strategies that may be used in translating Ariyoshi Sawako's novel *Ki no kawa* (1959; mentioned in previous chapters), which depicts its characters mainly according to their socially determined roles. A contemporary translator may choose to consciously retain this stratification for historical and narrative purposes or de-emphasize it so as to make the novel more "accessible" to contemporary readers. These two approaches represent options that the translator needs to weigh against translation goals. Translating without fully considering these issues, however, may result in inconsistent or unconsciously "skewed" translation, perhaps unintentionally foregrounding the translator's personal viewpoints or those of her culture as if they had been conscious choices resulting from a systematic approach.

Hermans has noted that "translations perhaps tell us more about those who translate than about the source text underlying the translation" (Hermans 1999: 59). In the case of unconscious ideology influencing one's translations and resulting in the unintentional appearance of noticeable subtexts in the work, this observation represents a negative phenomenon that can hopefully be minimized through greater awareness. The translator should have an awareness not only of ideological and social implications found in the source text but of how she herself desires to respond to these. It is only through noticing one's own viewpoints and seeing how they relate to the text that those viewpoints can be compensated for, if in fact such compensation is required.

Although seemingly an extraneous issue, **Financial Considerations** have the potential to negatively affect equivalence. In most cases, authors are the copyright holders for their works and so they (and by extension, their publishers) maintain *de facto* monopoly power over translations of these works. As such, the standards for assessing equivalence, until the copyright expires, are determined entirely by them. Aside from expecting that the translation will protect the author's "artistic integrity" and reputation in the public relations realm, equivalence under copyright will often include a strong dose of "financial equivalence." Put bluntly, do the profits resulting from the translation exceed the costs of having it produced and distributed. Noted Japanese translator Tanabe Teinosuke (1905-1984) has reflected on this particular type of equivalence:

I would like to consider the issue of arbitrary personal decisions that affect translation. One can consider such arbitrary personal decisions from two angles, that of the publisher and that of the translator. For a translated book to ever see the light of day, it is necessary for the arbitrary decisions of both parties to coincide. Nevertheless, the publisher's arbitrary decision is summed up by the expression, "This is gonna take off!" In fact, "take off" in this case simply means "likely to sell well." In other words, because at present publishing companies work entirely according to commercialism, a system based on the weak foundation of capitalism, everything comes down to whether it will "take off" or not. (Tanabe 1958: 13-14; Strack translation)

For this reason, although it is difficult to concretely define an "error" in literary translation generally, while the work is still under copyright, the definition is simple. An error is any problem with the translation that happens to cause headaches for the author or publisher. This may be true even if the translation is accurate in the commonly understood sense. In such situations, the translator no doubt will have an unstated desire not to cause trouble for anyone and thereby produce "errors." Once the copyright has expired, a new, much looser constraint system takes over.

When the waiting period is over, the translator, who until that point had been a more or less replaceable cog in the author's international distribution system, suddenly transforms into a full-fledged interpreter of the work. When the period designated for protection under copyright law ends, a sudden rush of translation often results, as was recently evidenced when the copyright for Antoine de Saint-Exupéry's *Le petit prince* (Saint-Exupéry 1943) expired in Japan and the work went into the public domain. (Japan's copyright protection currently extends 60 years after the author's death.) Between June and August of 2005, no less than four new translations of Saint-Exupéry's story made it into Japan's bookstores ("*Hoshi no ōjisama koerareru ka*"). It is not surprising that so many translators would be waiting for their chance to reinterpret a classic like *Le petit prince* In most cases, though, by the time the copyright has expired, much of the consumer demand has already dried up.

There is, however, a related issue that will negatively affect a literary work's equivalence even after it enters the public domain. This factor is **Lack of Historical Awareness of Translation Traditions** on the part of translators themselves. As chapter 7 in this book attests, the translation of literary works, and especially poetry, does not proceed in a vacuum. Poetry translators inevitably influence other poetry translators, both in broad terms of vision and approach and narrow terms of line-by-line technique and specific word choice. This influence is often haphazard and the lessons available from researching previous translations are not sufficiently internalized. To the extent that translators are aware of previous translations, there will always be room for incremental improvement, improvement as defined by subjective but nevertheless statistically verifiable criteria (cf. chapter 7).

The key advantage translators have with respect to the translation of literature is that language tends to change subtly over generations and greatly only over multiple generations. When translations of a specific literary work evolve at a rate of change faster than the surrounding linguistic context, improvement is assured. Unfortunately, in the current situation, with long copyright periods followed by a dramatic drop in interest in older works, conditions dictate that language and culture will change at a faster rate than translations will. As a result, copyrighted poetry in translation tends to seem linguistically stale.

In addition to being at the mercy of copyright limitations, to the extent that success is judged more in terms of profitability than proficiency, a high level of expertise alone will prove insufficient to guarantee a translator's professional reputation. Tanabe sums up the counterintuitive way that translator status is often established:

According to publishing companies, how well a translated book sells will be determined, first of all, based on whether it has masterpiece status, or if not a masterpiece, at least has had some media exposure, and secondly, the quality of the book's title. Who translated it or how well it has been translated are irrelevant. (Tanabe 1958: 18; Strack translation)

While it is undoubtedly true that the skill with which literary translators accomplish their extremely challenging task is not a skill that will usually be recognized by any but other translators working within the same languages, this seems not to be an ideal situation in which to promote translation and provide incentives for translators to improve their knowledge and skills. A need has been recognized to raise the status of translators to that of "qualified specialists on a par with physicians, lawyers, [and] architects" (Ulrych 2002: 296).

Media exposure may potentially help to alleviate some of this image problem. There are some translation traditions that even now seem to be improving the popular image of translators at least in the context of certain "classic" works. For example, recent years have seen a relative upsurge in media coverage for new translations of *Don Quijote de la Mancha* (Cervantes 1605) and translations of well-known works of Russian literature (e.g., Tolstoy 2000) by Richard Pevear and Larissa Volokhonsky (Mason).

Finally, I will point out one more factor that negatively affects equivalence, **Failure to Recognize the Blind Spots and Caprices of Human Attention**. Every child is sure that they know more than their parents and every translator is sure that the part of the text that attracts their attention is always the part that matters most. The key difference is that most children grow out of their naïveté, while many translators do not. This book is nothing if not an attempt to draw attention to the glacial yet powerful associational effects found in literature which fail to be reflected in translations precisely because they fail to capture the attention of translators.

As translators tie their lexical choices to specific translation goals, they are more capable of achieving the difficult compromises necessary to retain whatever elements of value that translator has perceived in the source text. Each of the factors that are mentioned as negatively affecting equivalence do so to the extent they interfere with the explicit goals of the translator and cause translators to overlook alternative salient features in the text.

According to civil engineering professor Henry Petroski, "[a]ll design involves conflicting objectives and hence compromise, and the best designs will always be those that come up with the best compromise" (Dembski 1999: 261). Literature that has not compromised some particular perceptional or associational cognitive aspects so as to accentuate some other cognitive aspects, risks failing to achieve anything memorable. In the same way, compromises in translation are inevitable and these compromises will undoubtedly result in some sort of literary, cultural, or linguistic loss.

Nevertheless, depending on the goals of the translator and the idiosyncrasies *of the specific text* being translated, translation at a high level of analogous meaning and analogous form that highlights that meaning is certainly possible. Having attempted to provide evidence for such a view of translation in this book's preceding chapters, the necessary groundwork has been laid to (at long last) offer a definition of translation: Translation is the process of interpreting a contextualized message in one language and reconstituting it in the context of another language so as to accomplish the goals of the translator. While this definition may be easiest to understand with respect to the translation of literature, the key role that translator objectives play even in more general kinds of translation have traditionally been overlooked and so the definition represents an attempt to explicitly recognize the fact that no translation is possible without at least a vague understanding of translator objectives.

Concerning Equivalence and Ethics in Translation

Translation is not a value-free activity. For this reason, ethical considerations are unavoidable. In concrete terms, because translation is a social activity and because the translator is in a relationship of relative power with respect to the majority of her non-bilingual readership, she therefore has a responsibility to aim for "neutrality" and "accuracy" (albeit defined and practiced on the translator's own terms) to the extent that the work has not been translated before. As translations abound and are freely available, however, the individual translator's power relationship with reference to the reader diminishes. As new translations appear and the monopoly held by the first translator of a work is displaced by multiple access points, the freedom to write for particular interpretive communities (cf. Fish 1980: 97-98) expands. To the extent that readers expect to be challenged, or surprised, or intrigued by a new interpretation of an old work, there is considerable license. To the extent that readers are encountering the work of another culture for the first time, the translator has a greater responsibility to remain aesthefically and ideologically neutral.

Nevertheless, personal ends will probably always play some role. Translation will thrive to the extent that it is simultaneously motivated by the broad goals of interpersonal and intercultural communication, the desire to share and receive reliable information, and the yearning to express what one feels to be essential at the expense of what is not. Japanese poet Takamura Kōtarō has summed up the translation of poetry in simple terms of polite consideration for others:

> In the end, the translation of poetry is nothing more than an expression of kindness. (Takamura 1921: 288; Strack translation)

Takamura's comment gives us one more metaphor with which to describe translation and it seems a simple yet valuable one. And yet the words "nothing more than" are a distraction. In this comment we again detect a hint of Shelley's conclusion about poetic translation, a conclusion that seems to be repeated over and over by poets (although not by translators). Shelley, Frost, Hagiwara, Takamura: the list goes on and on. In that poets are bound to have extremely exacting standards of equivalence, perhaps it is natural that they all believe that nothing of poetic consequence *to them* survives the translation process.

Is Translating Literature like Casting a Violet into a Crucible?

Shelley's metaphor is, to some extent, inapt. Violets can in fact be successfully analyzed to reveal their constituent chemicals. HPLC analysis has shown them to contain luteolin, apigenin, quercetin, hesperidin, ferulic acid, and ellagic acid among the flower's 40 odd phenolic compounds (Bubenchikov & Goncharov 2005). In short, while Shelley may be commended for producing a highly allusive and intuitively compelling metaphor, it seems unnecessarily inflexible to suggest that the only way to analyze the properties of a violet would be to cast it into a crucible and attempt to smelt it down. Furthermore, it might be stated that when poets like Frost and linguists like Jakobson make comments about how some "essential" aspect of poetry gets lost in translation or how the translation of poetry is "by definition" impossible, they are severely underrating both the talents of translators and the adaptive facility of literature.

Literature may be many things, but it is not a shrinking violet. Although it would be a blatant misstatement to say that nothing is lost in translation, it is equally incorrect to assert that nothing remains. Literature is not some cotton-candy confection that dissolves on contact with anything intensely pragmatic like translation. Literature, including poetry, is solid and substantial and essential precisely to the extent that human cognition is solid and substantial and essential.

While the challenge of translatability may not be the only challenge, or the ultimate challenge, for a literary work to live up to, it is one prominent challenge of our globalizing age. Furthermore, to the extent that literature is a form

202

of communication, literature that fails to communicate across cultures at a time during which a premium is placed on such interlingual covalency is, however many other positive attributes it may possess, under-adaptive. If Shelley's poetry had actually been as fragile as he himself made it out to be, I doubt that his name would still be remembered today. The fact that his imperfect analogy is still compelling even in the 21st century is, in fact, a kind of limited verification of literature's potential durability.

Translators should have a healthy respect for art, for language, for culture. Even the fear of failure is not necessarily a bad thing. All of these are capable of spurring the translator on toward success. There is no room, however, for the unthinking insistence that success in literary translation is, by definition, impossible. Neither should we passively submit to those who are afraid of putting literature to the test. Rest assured, some works will translate better than others. Those that do not translate well are likely to be valuable in a highly personal way to those who inhabit the author's particular linguistic and cultural viewpoint. Such viewpoints are worthwhile and should be defended but, ironically, the best way to defend a limited literary viewpoint is to translate it out to the world. In the end, especially for those who see timeless value in the particulars of local culture and view literature as something that unites rather than divides humanity, gold fears no fire.

REFERENCES

Abe Tamotsu. 1967. "*Ōgarasu.*" *Sekai no shi* 47: *Pō shishū.* Tokyo: Yayoi shobō. 9-17.

Alexieva, Bistra. 1993. "A Cognitive Approach to Translation Equivalence." *Translation as Social Action.* Ed. P. Zlateva. London: Routledge.

Ariyoshi Sawako. 1959. *Ki no kawa.* Tokyo: Shinchōsha, 2000.

Ariyoshi Sawako. 1981. *The River Ki.* Trans. Mildred Tahara. Tokyo: Kodansha.

Bamberg, Michael & Virginia Marchman. 1990. "What holds a narrative together? The linguistic encoding of episode boundaries." *Papers in Pragmatics,* 4(1). 58-122.

Bear, Mark F., Barry W. Connors & Michael A. Paradiso. 2001. *Neuroscience: Exploring the Brain,* 2nd Ed. Baltimore, MD: Lippincott Williams & Wilkins.

Bekku Sadanori. 1994. "*Koyū meishi wa kowai.*" In *Nihon no meizuihitsu, bekkan* 45: *Hon'yaku.* Ed. Bekku Sadanori. Tokyo: Sakuhinsha.

Bergen, Benjamin K. 2004. "The Psychological Reality of Phonaesthemes." *Language,* 80(2).

Berlin, Brent & Paul Kay. 1969. *Basic Color Terms: Their Universality and Evolution.* Berkeley: U of California P.

Bierce, Ambrose. 1890. "An Occurrence at Owl Creek Bridge." *The Complete Short Stories of Ambrose Bierce.* Ed. E.J. Hopkins. New York: Doubleday, 1970.

Bierce, Ambrose. 1969. "*Auru kurīkubashi no ichi jiken.*" Trans. Okuda Shunsuke. In *Biasu senshū,* vol. 1: *Sensō.* Tokyo: Tokyo Bijutsu. 25-42.

Bierce, Ambrose. 2000. "*Auru kurīku tekkyō de no dekigoto.*" Trans. Ōtsu Ei'ichirō. In *Biasu tanpenshū.* Ed. Ōtsu Ei'ichirō. Tokyo: Iwanami.

Blake, William. 1789. *Songs of Innocence.* In *Songs of Innocence and Experience.* Oxford: Oxford UP, 1970.

Blake, William. 1794. *Songs of Experience.* In *Songs of Innocence and Experience.* Oxford: Oxford UP, 1970.

Blasko, Dawn and Cynthia Connine. 1993. "Effects of familiarity and aptness on metaphor processing." *Journal of Experimental Psychology: Learning, Memory, and Cognition,* 19. 295-308.

Blasko, Dawn & Victoria Kazmerski. 2006. "ERP Correlates of Individual Differences in the Comprehension of Nonliteral Language." *Metaphor and Symbol*, 21(4). 267-284.

Booth, Wayne C. 1961. *The Rhetoric of Fiction*. Chicago: U of Chicago P.

Brooks, Richard, dir. 1954. *The Last Time I Saw Paris*. MGM.

Bubenchikov, R.A. & N.F. Goncharov. 2005. "HPLC Analysis of Phenolic Compounds in Field Violet." *Pharmaceutical Chemistry Journal*, 39(3). 143-144.

Carpenter, Humphrey. 1997. *The Inklings: C.S. Lewis, J.R.R. Tolkien, Charles Williams and their friends*. New York: HarperCollins.

Cervantes, Miguel de. 1605. "Don Quijote de la Mancha I." Ed. J.J. Allen. Madrid: Catedra, 2001.

Chandler, Raymond. 1997. *Raymond Chandler Speaking*. Eds. Dorothy Gardiner & Kathrine Sorley Walker. U of California P.

Clark, Eve V. 1973. How children describe time and order. *Studies of Child Language*. Eds. Charles A. Ferguson & Dan I. Slobin. New York: Holt, Rinehart & Winston. 586-606.

Conquest, Robert. 2004. "The Whys of Art." *The New Criterion*, 23(4). 5-14.

Conrad, Robert. 1902. *Heart of Darkness*. Harmondsworth: Penguin, 1973.

Conrad, Robert. 1958. *Yami no oku*. Trans. Nakano Yoshio. Tokyo: Iwanami.

Coulson, Seana. 2006. "Constructing Meaning." *Metaphor and Symbol*, 21(4). 245-266.

Croft, William & D. Alan Cruse. 2004. *Cognitive Linguistics*. Cambridge: Cambridge UP.

Cutler, Anne & Charles Clifton, Jr. 1999. In *The Neurocognition of Language*. Ed. Colin M. Brown & Peter Hagoort. Oxford: Oxford UP.

Damasio, Antonio. 1999. *The Feeling of What Happens: Body and Emotion in the Making of Consciousness*. San Diego, CA: Harcourt.

Damasio, Antonio. 2000. *Descartes' Error: Emotion, Reason and the Human Brain*. New York: Harper Collins.

Deacon, Terrance W. 1997. *The Symbolic Species: The Co-evolution of Language and the Brain*. New York: Norton.

Dembski, William. 1999. *Intelligent Design: The Bridge between Science and Theology*. Downers Grove, IL: Intervarsity.

Eco, Umberto. 2003. *Mouse or Rat? Translation as Negotiation*. London: Weidenfield & Nicolson.

Eco, Umberto. 2004. *On Literature*. Trans. Martin McLaughlin. Orlando, FL: Harcourt.

Edelman, Gerald. 1992. *Bright Air, Brilliant Fire: On the Matter of Mind*. New York: Basic Books.

Edelman, Gerald & Giulio Tononi. 2000. *A Universe of Consciousness*. New York: Basic

Books.

Emerson, Ralph Waldo. 1844. "The Poet." *Self-Reliance, and other essays.* New York: Dover, 1993.

Feldman, Jerome A. 2006. *From Molecules to Metaphor: A Neural Theory of Language.* Cambridge, MA: MIT P.

Fish, Stanley. 1980. *Is There a Text in This Class? The Authority of Interpretive Communities.* Cambridge, MA: Harvard UP.

Fitch, Noel Riley. 1989. *Walks in Hemingway's Paris.* New York: St. Martin's Griffin.

Fitzgerald, F. Scott. 1920. "May Day." *The Short Stories of F. Scott Fitzgerald.* New York: Scribners, 1989. 97-141.

Fitzgerald, F. Scott. 1925. *The Great Gatsby.* London: Penguin, 1994.

Fitzgerald, F. Scott. 1931. "Babylon Revisited." *The Short Stories of F. Scott Fitzgerald.* New York: Scribners, 1989. 616-633.

Fitzgerald, F. Scott. 1955. *"Ame no asa pari ni shisu."* Trans. Shimizu Kō. Tokyo: Mikasa Shinsho.

Fitzgerald, F. Scott. 1957a. *Karei naru gyattsubī.* Trans. Ōnuki Saburō. Tokyo: Kadokawa.

Fitzgerald, F. Scott. 1957b. *Idai naru gyattsubī.* Trans. Nozaki Takashi. Tokyo: Kenkyusha.

Fitzgerald, F. Scott. 1992a. *"Mei dei."* Fuittsujerarudo tanpenshū. Trans. Saeki Yasuki. Tokyo: Iwanami. 325-370.

Fitzgerald, F. Scott. 1992b. *"Babiron saihō."* Fuittsujerarudo tanpenshū. Trans. Saeki Yasuki. Tokyo: Iwanami. 87-194.

Fitzgerald, F. Scott. 1999. *"Babiron ni kaeru."* Trans. Murakami Haruki. Tokyo: Chuō kō-ronsha.

Fitzgerald, Scott. 2006. *Za gurēto gyattsubī.* Trans. Murakami Haruki. Tokyo: Chuo kōron shinsha

Fludernik, Monika, Donald C. Freeman & Margaret H. Freeman. 1999."Metaphor and Beyond: An Introduction." *Poetics Today,* 20(3). 383-396.

Freedman, Monica L. & Randi C. Martin. 2001. "Dissociable components of short-term memory and their relation to long-term learning." *Cognitive Neuropsychology,* 18-3.

Freeman, Margaret. 2002. "The body in the word: A cognitive approach to the shape of a poetic text." *Cognitive Stylistics: Language and Cognition in Text Analysis.* Eds. Elena Semino & Jonathan Culpepper. Amsterdam: John Benjamins. 23-47.

Frye, Northrop. 1990. "The Expanding World of Metaphor." In *Northrop Frye: Myth and Metaphor, Selected Essays,* 1974-1988. Ed. Robert D. Denham. Charlottesville: UP of Virginia.

Fukunaga Takehiko. 1970. "*Karasu*." *Pō zenshū*, 3. Tokyo: Sōgensha. 142-148.

Futabatei Shimei. 1887. *Ukigumo*. Tokyo: Iwanami Shoten, 1941.

Futabatei Shimei. 1967. *Ukigumo*. Trans. Marleigh Grayer Ryan. *Japan's First Modern Novel: Ukigumo of Futabatei Shimei*. New York: Columbia UP.

García Lorca, Federico. 1987. "*Ciudad sin Sueño (Nocturno del Brooklyn Bridge)*." *Yerma, Poeta en Nueva York*. Barcelona: Biblioteco de Bolsillo.

García Lorca, Federico. 1990. "Sleepless City (Brooklyn Bridge Nocturne)." *Poet in New York*. London: Penguin.

Gibbs, Raymond W. 1994. *The Poetics of Mind: Figurative Thought, Language, and Understanding*. Cambridge: Cambridge UP.

Gioia, Dana. 2004. *Disappearing Ink: Poetry at the End of Print Culture*. Saint Paul, MN: Graywolf.

Givón, Thomas. 1985. "Iconicity, isomorphism and non-arbitrary coding in syntax." *Iconicity in Syntax*. Ed. John Haiman. Amsterdam: John Benjamins. 187-220.

Goethe, Johann Wolfgang von. 1827. *The Columbia World of Quotations*. New York: Columbia UP, 1996.

Haga Tōru, ed. 2000. *Hon'yaku to Nihon bunka*. Tokyo: *Kokusai bunka kōryū suishin kyō kai*.

Hagiwara Sakutarō. 1917a. "*Jo*." *Hagiwara Sakutarō zenshū*, vol. 1. Tokyo: Chikuma Shobō 1975. 10-14.

Hagiwara Sakutarō. 1917b. "*Take*." *Hagiwara Sakutarō zenshū*, vol. 1. Tokyo: Chikuma Shobō, 1975. 21-22.

Hagiwara Sakutarō. 1933. "*Shi no hon'yaku ni tsuite*." *Hagiwara Sakutarō zenshū*, vol. 9. Tokyo: Chikuma Shobō, 1976. 88-98.

"Harry Blackstone, Sr." *Wikipedia*. 26 Nov. 2006.
  <http://en.wikipedia.org/wiki/Harry_Blackstone,_Sr.>

Hebb, Donald. 1949. *The Organization of Behavior: A Neuropsychological Theory*. New York: Wiley.

Hemingway, Ernest. 1929. *A Farewell to Arms*. New York: Scribners.

Hemingway, Ernest. 1940. *For Whom the Bell Tolls*. New York: Simon & Schuster.

Hemingway, Ernest. 1951. *Buki yo saraba*. Trans. Ōkubo Yasuo. Tokyo: Mikasa Shobō.

Hemingway, Ernest. 1994. *Ta ga tame ni kane wa naru: gekan*. Trans. Ōkubo Yasuo. Tokyo: Shinchōsha.

Herbert, George. 1880. "Easter Wings." In *Metaphor and Iconicity: A Cognitive Approach to Analysing Texts*. Hiraga, Masako K. New York: Palgrave Macmillan, 2005. 58-59.

Hermans, Theo. 1999. "Translation and Normativity." In *Translation and Norms.* Ed. C. Schäffner. Clevedon: Multilingual Matters. 50-71.

Hinatsu Kōnosuke. 1935. "*Ōkarasu.*" *Pō shishū.* Tokyo: Sōgensha, 1950. 117-130.

Hiraga, Masako K. 2005. *Metaphor and Iconicity: A Cognitive Approach to Analysing Texts.* New York: Palgrave Macmillan.

Horiguchi Daigaku. 1958. "*Hon'yaku koborebanashi.*" In *Nihon-no meizuihitsu, bekkan* 45: *Honyaku.* Ed. Bekku Sadanori. Tokyo: Sakuhinsha, 1994.

"*Hoshi no ōjisama koerareru ka.*" [Can *The Little Prince* be improved upon?] *Yomiuri Shimbun* [newspaper]. 2 Aug. 2005. 15.

House, Juliane. 2002. "Universality versus culture specificity in translation." In *Translation Studies: Perspecitves on an Emerging Discipline.* Ed. Alessandra Riccardi. Cambridge: Cambridge UP. 92-110.

Innis, Robert E. 1985. *Semiotics: An Introductory Anthology.* Bloomington: Indiana UP.

Jakobson, Roman. 1956. "Two Aspects of Language and Two Types of Aphasic Disturbances." In Jakobson, Roman & Morris Halle. *Fundamentals of Language.* The Hague: Mouton.

Jakobson, Roman. 1959. "On Linguistic Aspects of Translation." Rpt. in *Language in Literature.* Ed. Krystyna Pomorska & Stephen Rudy. Cambridge, MA: Harvard UP, 1987.

Jakobson, Roman. 1960. "Linguistics and Poetics." *Style in Language.* Cambridge, MA: MIT P. 350-377.

James, Henry. 1964. "The Figure in the Carpet." In *The Complete Tales of Henry James.* Ed. L. Edel. London: Rupert Hart-Davies. 273-315.

Johnson, Samuel. 1781. *Lives of the English Poets,* vol. 1: *Milton.* Tokyo: Kenkyusha, 1949.

Joyce, James. 1922. *Ulysses.* Paris: Shakespeare and Company.

Kafka, Franz. 1915. *The Metamorphosis.* London: Bantam, 1972.

Kajima Shōzō. 1997. "*Ōgarasu.*" *Pō shishū: taiyaku.* Tokyo: Iwanami. 141-161.

Kajiyama Ken. 1979. *Sekai in'yōku jiten.* Tokyo: Meiji Shoin.

Kay, Paul & Willett Kempton. "What is the Sapir-Whorf Hypothesis?" *American Anthropologist,* 86: 65-79.

Keene, Donald. 1984. *Dawn to the West: Japanese Literature of the Modern Era.* New York: Holt.

Kehler, Andrew. 2002. *Coherence, Reference, and the Theory of Grammar.* Stanford, CA: CSLI Publications.

Kennedy, X.J. & Dana Gioia. 2002. *Literature: An Introduction to Fiction, Poetry, and Drama (8th Ed.).* New York: Longman.

Kimmel, Michael. 2005. "From Metaphor to the "Mental Sketchpad": Literary Macrostructure and Compound Image Schemas." *Metaphor and Symbol*, 20(3). 199-238.

Kipling, Rudyard. 1898. "The Bridge-Builders." *The Day's Work.* Oxford: Oxford UP, 1987. 5-37.

Kipling, Rudyard. 1995. "*Hashi wo tsukuru mono tachi.*" Trans. Hashimoto Makinori. Kipuringu Tanpenshū. Ed. Hashimoto Makinori. Tokyo: Iwanami Shoten. 129-182.

"Kishū-ben" *Wikipedia.* 28 Dec. 2006. <http://ja.wikipedia.org/wiki/>

Kitamura Masaru. 2000. "*Hon'yaku to gaikō.*" In *Hon'yaku to Nihon bunka.* Ed. Haga Tōru Tokyo: *Kokusai bunka kōryū suishin kyōkai.*

Koller, Werner. 1992. *Einführung in die Übersetzunqswissenschaft.* Heidelberg: Quelle & Meyer.

Koster, Cees. 2002. "The Translator Between the Texts: On the Textual Presence of the Translator as an issue of Methodology of Comparative Translation Description." *Translation Studies: Perspectives on an Emerging Discipline.* Ed. Alessandra Riccardi. Cambridge: Cambridge UP.

Kōtoku Shūsui. 1994. "*Honyaku no kushin.*" In *Nihon no meizuihitsu, bekkan* 45: *Hon'yaku.* Ed. Bekku Sadanori. Tokyo: Sakuhinsha.

Kutas, Marta. 2006. "One Lesson Learned: Frame Language Processing—Literal and Figurative—as a Human Brain Function." *Metaphor and Symbol*, 21(4). 285-325.

Kyūyaku seisho: Kōgoyaku. (Holy Bible, New Testament: Japanese Colloquial Translation) 1955. Tokyo: Nihon Seisho Kyōkai.

Lakoff, George. 1987. Women, Fire and Dangerous Things. Chicago: U of Chicago P.

Lakoff, George. 1993. "The Contemporary Theory of Metaphor." In Ed. Andrew Ortony. *Metaphor and Thought*, 2nd Ed. Cambridge: Cambridge UP. 202-251.

Lakoff, George. 1996. *Moral Politics: What Conservatives Know that Liberals Don't.* Chicago: U of Chicago P.

Lakoff, George & Mark Johnson. 1980. *Metaphors We Live By.* Chicago: U of Chicago P.

Lakoff, George & Mark Johnson. 1999. *Philosophy in the Flesh.* New York: Basic Books.

Lakoff, George & Mark Turner. 1989. *More than Cool Reason: A Field Guide to Poetic Metaphor.* Chicago: U of Chicago P.

Lamb, Sydney M. 1998. *Pathways of the Brain: The Neurocognitive Basis of Langauge.* Amsterdam: John Benjamins.

Lappin, Shalom & Herbert Leass. 1994. "An algorithm for pronominal anaphora resolution." *Computational Linguistics*, 20: 535-561.

Lennon, John & Paul McCartney. 1965. "Norwegian Wood (This Bird Has Flown)." *Rubber*

REFERENCES *209*

Soul. London: Parlophone.

Lewis, C.S. 1967a. *Studies in Words*, 2nd Ed. Cambridge: Cambridge UP.

Lewis, C.S. 1967b. "The Language of Religion." *Christian Reflections*. New York: Inspirational Press, 1991.

Lodge, David. 1977. *The Modes of Modern Writing: Metaphor, Metonymy, and the Typology of Modern Literature*. New York: Cornell UP.

Maalej, Zouhair. 2006. "Figurative Language in Anger Expressions in Tunisian Arabic: An Extended View of Embodiment." *Metaphor and Symbol*, 19(1). 51-75

MacAndrew, Andrew R. 1981. "A Note from the Translator." In Fyodor Dostoevsky. 1880. *The Brothers Karamazov*. Trans. Andrew R. MacAndrew. New York: Bantam, 1981. x.

Martindale, Colin.1990. *The Clockwork Muse: The Predictability of Artistic Change*. New York: Basic Books.

Mason, Ian G. "Don of a New Era: 'The Sloppiest Masterpiece in Existence' gets translated — for the umpteenth time." *National Post*. 15 Nov. 2003. <http://www.nationalpost.com>

Masuda Koh, ed. 1974. *Kenkyusha's New Japanese English Dictionary*, 4th Ed. Tokyo: Kenkyusha.

Matsuo Bashō. 1702. *Oku no Hosomichi*. Rpt. in *The Narrow Road to Oku*. Trans. Donald Keene. Tokyo: Kodansha International, 1996.

Matsuo Bashō. 1966. *The Narrow Road to the Deep North and other travel sketches*.Trans. Nobuyuki Yuasa. London: Penguin.

Matsuo Bashō. 1974. *A Haiku Journey: Bashō's Narrow Road to a Far Province*. Trans. Dorothy Britton. Tokyo: Tuttle.

Matsuo Bashō. 1976. *Bashō zenkushū*. Eds. Inui Hiroyuki, Sakurai Takejirō & Nagano Hitoshi. Tokyo: Ōfū.

Matsuo Bashō. 1996. *The Narrow Road to Oku*. Trans. Donald Keene. Tokyo: Kodansha International.

Matter Mandler, Jean. 2004. *The Foundations of Mind: Origins of Conceptual Thought*. Oxford: Oxford UP.

Maupassant, Guy de. 1987a. "Apparition." *Apparition, et autres contes d'angoisse*. Paris: Garnier Flammarion.

Maupassant, Guy de. 1987b. "*Yūrei*." Trans. Okamoto Kidō. *Sekai kaidan meisaku shū*, vol. 2. Tokyo: Kawade.

Maupassant, Guy de. 2002. "The Apparition." In *Original Short Stories*, vol. 7. Trans. Albert M.C. McMaster, A.E. Henderson & Louise C.J. Quesada. Boston, MA: IndyPublish. 112-

118.

Mishima Yukio. 1956. "Hashizukushi." *Mishima Yukio Zenshū*, vol. 10. Tokyo: Shinchōsha, 1973.

Mishima Yukio. 1966. "The Seven Bridges." In Mishima Yukio. *Death in Midsummer and Other Stories*. Trans. Donald Keene. New York: New Directions.

Miyamoto Teru. 1978. *Doro-no kawa*. In *Hotarugawa, Doro no kawa*. Tokyo: Shinchō Bunko, 1994.

Miyamoto Teru. 1991. "Muddy River." In *River of Fireflies*. Trans. Ralph McCarthy. Tokyo: Kodansha International.

Moretti, Franco. 1999. *Atlas of the European Novel*. London: Verso.

Morgan, B.Q. 1966. "A critical bibliography of works on translation." *On Translation*. Ed. R.A. Brower. New York: Oxford UP. 271-293.

Murakami Haruki. 1991. *Noru'uei no mori*, vol. 1. Tokyo: Kōdansha.

Murakami Haruki. 1997. *The Wind-up Bird Chronicle*. Trans. Jay Rubin. New York: Knopf.

Murakami Haruki. 1999. *South of the Border, West of the Sun*. Trans. Philip Gabriel. New York: Knopf.

Murakami Haruki. 2000. *Norwegian Wood*. Trans. Jay Rubin. New York: Vintage.

Murakami Haruki. 2005. *Kafka on the Shore*. Trans. Philip Gabriel. New York: Vintage.

Nagai Kafū. 1909. "*Botan no kyaku*." *Kafū Zenshū*, vol. 4. Iwanami Shoten, 1964. 71-84.

Nagai Kafū. 1972. "The Peony Garden." *A Strange Tale from East of the River and Other Stories*. Trans. Edward Seidensticker. Tokyo: Tuttle.

Nakano Michio. 1994. *Hon'yaku wo kangaeru: Nihongo no sekai, eigo no sekai*. Tokyo: Sanseidō.

Natsume Sōseki. 1911. "*Henna oto*." In *Omoidasu koto nado, hoka nanapen*. Tokyo: Iwanami, 1986. 140-147.

Nida, Eugene A. & Charles Taber. 1969. *The Theory and Practice of Translation*. Leiden: Brill.

O'Regan, J. Kevin, Ronald A. Rensick & Jame J. Clark. 1999. "Change-blindness as a result of mudsplashes." *Nature* 398(6722).

Paivio, A. 1971. *Imagery and Verbal Processes*. New York: Holt, Rhinehart & Winston.

Perloff, Marjorie. 2006. "The Poetry-Sound Initiative: A Convention Preview." *MLA Newsletter*, 38(3).

Pinker, Stephen. 2002. *The blank slate: The modern denial of human nature*. New York: Viking.

Poe, Edgar Allan. 1845. "The Raven." *The Complete Works of Edgar Allan Poe*. New York:

AMS Press, 1965. 94-100.

Poe, Edgar Allan. 1846. "The Philosophy of Composition." *Selections from the Critical Writings of Edgar Allan Poe.* Ed. F.C. Prescott. New York: Gordian Press, 1981.

Poe, Edgar Allan. 1850. "The Poetic Principle." *Selections from the Critical Writings of Edgar Allan Poe.* Ed. F.C. Prescott. New York: Gordian Press, 1981.

Popova, Yanna. 2002. "The Figure in the Carpet: Discovery or Re-cognition." *Cognitive Stylistics: Language and Cognition in Text Analysis.* Eds. Elena Semino & Jonathan Culpepper. Amsterdam: John Benjamins. 49-71.

Rabassa, Gregory. 2005. *If This Be Treason: Translation and Its Discontents.* New York: New Directions.

Regier, Terry. 1996. *The Human Semantic Potential.* Cambridge, MA: MIT P.

Reynolds, Michael. 1976. *Hemingway's First War.* Princeton: Princeton UP.

Rimbaud, Arthur. 1886. *Illuminations.* Geneva: Droz, 1969.

Rossetti, Dante Gabriel. 1992. "Preface to *The Early Italian Poets.*" In *Theories of Translation: An Anthology of Essays from Dryden to Derrida.* Eds. Rainer Schulte & John Biguenet. Chicago: U of Chicago P.

Rubin, Jay. Interview. "Haruki *no yomarekata*" *Yomiuri Shimbun* (newspaper), 5 Apr. 2006. 14.

Saijō Yaso. 1927. "Ōgarasu." *Saijō Yaso Zenshū.* Tokyo: Kokusho Kankōkai, 1995. 108-114.

Saint-Exupéry, Antoine de. 1943. *Le petit prince.* Paris: Gallimard, 1999.

Satō Hiroaki. *Basho's Narrow Road.* Berkeley, CA: Stonebridge.

Scarpa, Federica. 2002. "Closer and closer apart: Specialized translation in a cognitive perspective." *Translation Studies: Perspectives on an Emerging Discipline.* Ed. Alessandra Riccardi. Cambridge: Cambridge UP. 133-149.

Schäffner, Christina. 2004. "Metaphor and translation: some implications of a cognitive approach." *Journal of Pragmatics,* 36. 1253-1269.

Schopenhauer, Arthur. 1992. "On Language and Words" in *Theories of Translation: An Anthology of Essays from Dryden to Derrida.* Eds. Rainer Schulte & John Biguenet. Chicago: U of Chicago P. 32-35.

Schulte, Rainer and John Biguenet. 1992. *Theories of Translation: An Anthology of Essays from Dryden to Derrida.* Chicago: U of Chicago P.

Schwartz, Debora. "Shakespearean Verse and Prose." 7 Jan. 2007. <http://cola.calpoly.edu/~dschwart/engl339/verseprose.html>

Semino, Elena & Jonathan Culpepper. 2002. "Foreword." *Cognitive Stylistics: Language and Cognition in Text Analysis.* Eds. Elena Semino & Jonathan Culpepper. Amsterdam: John

Benjamins.

Shelley, Percy Bysshe. 1821. "A Defence of Poetry, Part First" in *The Complete Works of Percy Bysshe Shelley: Prose*, vol. VII. New York: Gordian Press, 1965.

Shimada Kinji. 1969. "*Karasu.*" *Sekai meishishū*, 21. Tokyo: Heibonsha. 6-12.

Shinmura Izuru, ed. 1991. *Kōjien*, 4th Ed. Tokyo: Iwanami.

Shinyaku seisho: Kōgoyaku. (Holy Bible, New Testament: Japanese Colloquial Translation) 1954. Tokyo: Nihon Seisho Kyōkai.

Shirakawa Yōji. 2003. Personal Interview.

Simpsons, The (Japanese voice-over track). 2005. Dir. David Silverman. Season 2, Episode 3 (Series Episode 16). DVD, 20th Century Fox Home Entertainment Japan.

Simpsons, The (Japanese subtitles). 2005. Dir. David Silverman. Season 2, Episode 3 (Series Episode 16). DVD, 20th Century Fox Home Entertainment Japan.

Smyth, Ron. 1994. "Grammatical determinants of ambiguous pronoun resolution." *Journal of Psycholinguistic Research*, 23(3): 197-229.

Snel Trampus, Rita D. 2002. "Aspects of a theory of norms and some issues in teaching translation." In *Translation Studies: Perspecitves on an Emerging Discipline.*Ed. Alessandra Riccardi. Cambridge: Cambridge UP. 38-54.

Snell-Hornby, Mary 1983. "Metaphorical Thought and Translation: Taking a Stand on P. Newmark." Duisburg: L.A.U.T. Series A 108.

Snell-Hornby, Mary 1988. *Translation Studies: An Integrated Approach.* Amsterdam: John Benjamins.

Steiner, George. 1998. *After Babel: Aspects of Language and Translation*, 3rd Ed. Oxford: Oxford UP.

Stockwell, Peter. 2002. "Miltonic texture and the feeling of reading." In *Cognitive Stylistics: Language and Cognition in Text Analysis.* Eds. Elena Semino & Jonathan Culpepper. Amsterdam: John Benjamins. 73-94.

Stockwell, Peter. 2002. *Cognitive Poetics: an introduction.* London: Routledge.

Strack, Daniel C. 2000. "Hemingway's Hidden Agenda in *For Whom the Bell Tolls.*" *The University of Kitakyushu Faculty of Humanities Journal*, 59. Kitakyushu: The University of Kitakyushu. 97-127.

Strack, Daniel C. 2002. "Theories of Learning in Applied Linguistics: A Neurobiological Perspective." *Waseda University Institute of Language Teaching Journal*, 57. Tokyo: Waseda University. 1-31.

Strack, Daniel C. 2004. "The Bridge Project: Research on Metaphor, Culture and Cognition." *The University of Kitakyushu Faculty of Humanities Journal*, 68. 19-45.

Strack, Daniel C. 2006a. "Who are the Bridge Builders? Metaphor, Metonymy and the Architecture of Empire." *Style*, 39(1). 39-54.

Strack, Daniel C. 2006b. "When the PATH OF LIFE crosses the RIVER OF TIME: Multivalent Bridge Metaphor in Literary Contexts." *The University of Kitakyushu Faculty of Humanities Journal*, 72. 1-18.

Sweetser, Eve. 1990. *From Etymology to Pragmatics: Metaphorical and cultural aspects of semantic change.* Cambridge: Cambridge UP.

Tabakowska, Elzbieta. 1993. *Cognitive Linguistics and Poetics of Translation.* Tübingen: Narr.

Takachi Jun'ichiro. 2004. Unpublished research paper. "*Bashō no eiyaku to Keishō to Gūi*" (Translation of Bashō's Haiku and Figures & Allegories). Japan Comparative Literature Association National Conference. Tōyō University, Tokyo. 27 Jun. 2004.

Takahashi Yoshitaka. 1952. "*Henshin-ni tsuite.*" In Franz Kafka. *Henshin.* Trans. Takahashi Noritaka. Tokyo: Shinchōsha.

Takamura Kōtarō. 1921. "*Akarui toki: jobun.*" *Takamura Kōtarō Zenshū*, vol. 8. Tokyo: Chikuma Shobō, 1996. 288-289.

Tanabe Teinosuke. 1958. "*Hon'yaku zakkan.*" In *Nihon-no meizuihitsu, bekkan* 45: *Hon'yaku.* Ed. Bekku Sadanori. Tokyo: Sakuhinsha, 1994. 10-22.

Tanizaki Seiji. 1970. "*Ōgarasu.*" *Edogā Aran Pō Zenshū*, 6. Tokyo: Shunjūsha. 7-16.

Taylor, James. 1976. "Shower the People." *In the Pocket.* CD, Warner Brothers.

"The Great Leon, (Leon Levy)." *Bios of Famous Members— IBM Ring #21.* 26 Nov. 2006. <http://www.ibmring21.org/famous.html>

Thomas, Francis Noël & Mark Turner. 1994. *Clear and Simple as the Truth: Writing Classic Prose.* Princeton: Princeton UP.

Tolstoy, Leo. 1961. *Anna Karenina.* Trans. David Magarshack. New York: Signet.

Tolstoy, Leo. 1983. *Anna Karenina.* Trans. Louise Maude & Aylmer Maude. Oxford: Oxford UP.

Tolstoy, Leo. 2000. *Anna Karenina.* Trans. Richard Pevear & Larissa Volokhonsky. New York: Penguin.

Tomasello, Michael. 1999. *The Cultural Origins of Human Cognition.* Cambridge, MA: Harvard UP.

Tomasello, Michael & Josep Call. 1997. *Primate Cognition.* Oxford: Oxford UP.

Tsur, Reuven. 1998. *Poetic Rhythm: Structure and Performance— An Empirical Study in Cognitive Linguistics.* Bern: Peter Lang.

Tsur, Reuven. 2002. "Aspects of Cognitive Poetics." *Cognitive Stylistics: Language and*

Cognition in Text Analysis. Eds. Elena Semino & Jonathan Culpepper. Amsterdam: John Benjamins.

Tuggy, David. 1993. "Ambiguity, polysemy, and vagueness." *Cognitive Linguistics*, 4(3). 273-290.

Turgenev, Ivan. 1862. *Fathers and Sons.* New York: Norton, 1966.

Twain, Mark. (1890) 1992. *Collected Tales, Sketches, Speeches, & Essays: 1852-1890.* New York: Library of America.

Ueda Makoto. 1970. *Matsuo Bashō.* Tokyo: Tuttle.

Ulrych, Margherita. 2002. "An Evidence-based Approach to Applied Translation Studies." *Translation Studies: Perspecitves on an Emerging Discipline.* Ed. Alessandra Riccardi. Cambridge: Cambridge UP. 198-213.

Untermeyer, Louis. 1965. *Bygones: The Recollections of Louis Untermeyer.* Harcourt, Brace & World.

Valéry, Paul. 1992. "Variations on the *Eclogues.*" In *Theories of Translation: An Anthology of Essays from Dryden to Derrida.* Eds. Rainer Schulte and John Biguenet. Chicago: U of Chicago P. 113-126.

Van Peer, Willie. 1986. *Stylistics and Psychology: Investigations of Foregrounding.* New York: Croom Helm.

Walford, John. 2002. *Great Themes in Art.* Upper Saddle River, NJ: Prentice-Hall.

Watanabe Shōichi. 1992. *Kotoba konseputo jiten.* Tokyo: Dai-ichi Hōki Shuppan.

Weise, Günter. 1994. "Stages in the comprehension of scientific texts." *Fachsprache International Journal of LSP*, 16(3-4). 98-105.

Werth, Paul. 1994. "Extended Metaphor: a text world account." Language and Literature, 3(2). 79-103.

Yamasaki Kōtarō. 2000. *"Eiga jimaku no sekai to hon'yakusha: ichibyō yonmoji no ketsudan."* In *Hon'yaku to Nihon bunka.* Ed. Haga Tōru. Tokyo: *Kokusai bunka kōryū suishin kyōkai.* 140-149.

Yamauchi Shigekatsu. "No language better than others." *The Daily Yomiuri.* 6 Dec. 2005 2005: 17.

■ About the Author

Daniel C. Strack is a Professor in the English Department at the University of Kitakyushu, Kitakyushu, Japan. He teaches Japanese to English translation, English composition, and American culture. His research areas include Japanese literature, comparative literature, metaphor theory, and translation studies. He received his Ph.D. in Societal and Cultural Comparison from Kyushu University in 2013.

LITERATURE IN THE CRUCIBLE OF TRANSLATION: A COGNITIVE ACCOUNT (REVISED SECOND EDITION)

2007年 3 月30日　初版第 1 刷発行
2016年 4 月20日　第 2 版第 1 刷発行

■著　　者──ダニエル・ストラック
■発 行 者──佐藤　守
■発 行 所──株式会社**大学教育出版**
　　　　　　〒700 - 0953　岡山市南区西市855 - 4
　　　　　　電話(086)244 - 1268代　FAX (086)246 - 0294
■印刷製本──モリモト印刷㈱
■装　　丁──ダニエル・ストラック、ティーボーンデザイン事務所

Ⓒ Daniel C. Strack 2016, Printed in Japan
検印省略　　落丁・乱丁本はお取り替えいたします。
本書のコピー・スキャン・デジタル化等の無断複製は著作権法上での例外を除き禁じられています。本書を代行業者等の第三者に依頼してスキャンやデジタル化することは、たとえ個人や家庭内での利用でも著作権法違反です。

ISBN978 - 4 - 86429 - 391 - 4